Country Egg, City Egg

Country Egg, City Egg

Gayle Pirie and John Clark

Illustrations by Rollin McGrail

Artisan • New York

Published by Artisan

A Division of Workman Publishing, Inc.

708 Broadway

New York, New York 10003

www.workman.com

Library of Congress Cataloging-in-Publication Data

Pirie, Gayle

   Country egg, city egg / Gayle Pirie and John Clark.

     p. cm.

   Includes index.

   ISBN 1-57965-151-8

    1. Cookery (Eggs) I. Clark, John, 1959– II. Title.

TX745 .P57 2000

641.675—dc21   99-056347

Printed in Canada

10 9 8 7 6 5 4 3 2 1

Book design by LeAnna Weller and Dania Davey

For little Magnus

Acknowledgments

Our appreciation goes to the following friends who have given their time and talents to this book: Patricia Curtan for indispensable insight, Molly Sullivan and Amaryll Schwertner for their recipe contribution, and Diana Howard for finding us six years ago. And to Judy Rodgers for giving us the opportunity to create egg dishes at Zuni, to our editors at Artisan for having faith in this book, and to Rollin McGrail for her charming illustrations. A special thank-you to our friends and family for watching Magnus, allowing us to write this book.

Contents

Before You Crack

The yearning for basic pleasures, like eating well, takes on more urgency in our complex and technological world. Individuals, couples, and families long to slow down their hectic pace and savor the moment that a simple delicious meal affords. It was this thought that inspired us to write *Country Egg, City Egg*. Eggs are the ultimate and purest fast food on the planet, and when we peruse the refrigerator and discover a dozen eggs, how rich we are! Nourishment is just a few minutes away, the meal possibilities endless.

Though our affair with eggs started with writing brunch menus at the Zuni Café in San Francisco, the recipes in this book reflect the meals we cook at home for our family, friends, and ourselves. As you might expect, there is many a great breakfast and brunch dish here, but others—like Flash-Fried Eggs (page 97) and Ale and Cheddar Omelet (page 73)—appeal for lunch, supper, or late-night repasts.

Eggs are for us a medium through which we achieve thoughtful and winning combinations that satisfy anytime, any day. *Country Egg, City Egg* is about an approach to eating well, with splendid little meals, without a lot of fuss and lead time.

The Virtuous, Newly Laid Egg

The freshest eggs are worth foraging for. We favor purchasing eggs from our local farmers' markets, whose suppliers provide eggs from chickens that lead healthy lives. Fresh eggs have firm golden yolks surrounded by clear, viscous, clinging whites.

You can use either white or brown eggs. Eggshell color is a distinction not of quality, but of chicken variety. Reddish-brown hens produce brown eggs; white hens lay white eggs. The age of the chicken determines the size of the egg. The older the hen, the larger the egg. Large Grade AA eggs, which are the size used in our recipes, come from a chicken approximately one year old. Before eggs come to market, each egg is examined for quality through a lighting system that details the thickness of the egg white. Slight variations in the thickness distinguish the A from the AA; substandard readings generate a B grade, an egg not common in American consumer markets.

Eggs stay fresher longer the colder they are kept. Though you can store eggs up to three weeks, use them sooner than later; the longer eggs are stored, the more their purity and performance are compromised. Keep eggs refrigerated and in their carton, sealed off from other foods that smell. Their porous shells absorb odors, a virtue only when eggs mingle with an intoxicating fresh black truffle.

The Earnest Gesture—Rolling the Omelet

An omelet is a gift really, because of pure ingredients and honest presentation. Use a 7- or 8-inch nonstick pan or seasoned omelet pan. The high-angled handle of an omelet pan helps in rolling the omelet, but the pan requires time to season. A nonstick pan has a straight handle, but the instant nonstick surface is ready to go. Wipe out both types of "egg pan" with a soft kitchen towel to protect their surfaces.

Omelets require brisk cooking over medium-high heat. Heat the pan thoroughly before adding the eggs, using 1 tablespoon of butter per omelet. While the butter melts, lightly beat the eggs in a bowl—too many air bubbles whipped into the eggs will cause the omelet to dry out—and season with salt to taste. After the butter foams, but before it turns brown, add the eggs to the pan. The egg mixture will begin to set on the bottom within 30 seconds. Begin to pull in the sides with a wooden spoon, spatula, fork, or chopstick to allow the raw egg to run underneath the thin sheet of cooked egg. Repeat this step two or three times until most of the egg bottom is set, while the surface remains moist and creamy. This is the time to place your filling onto the egg. Tilt the pan forward, forcing the egg against the side of the pan. Start to roll the cooked side of the eggs over the creamy side—and the filling, if you've added it. Repeat the rolling gesture quickly until the cooked side has rolled back upon itself to create a plump oval seared on the outside with creamy layers within. A classic finish to an omelet is to draw a piece of sweet butter over its surface.

A Word About Poaching and Steaming

To poach eggs, you will need a straight-sided heavy sauté pan or pot filled with 2 to 3 inches of simmering water, a slotted spoon, and a kitchen towel. The water should never boil, because excess heat will cause eggs to rupture in the water and toughen the egg whites. Crack the eggs one at a time into a bowl and slide each egg into the simmering water. Add a tiny pinch of salt or a few drops of mild vinegar or lemon juice to the water to help set the egg white. However, if you are using very fresh eggs—thick egg whites clinging to vibrant yolks—such additions are unnecessary.

Into gently simmering water, add eggs one at a time and allow 3 minutes for them to set. Turn each egg once or twice in the water for even cooking. Add 30 seconds to 2 minutes more cooking time, depending on the desired doneness. The eggs should not cook for more than 5 minutes. Remove the eggs with a slotted spoon and blot excess water gently on a towel. Trim the edges of the eggs for a neater appearance. They can be served immediately, or refrigerated for several hours.

To steam eggs, use an egg steamer pan, which has nonstick eggcups supported by an insert to put over the boiling water. Or create your own egg steamer by using a simple metal vegetable steamer in a deep pot with a tight-fitting lid and nonstick eggcups or small ramekins. Butter each eggcup, then crack an egg into it and place into the steamer. Cover and allow 3 to 5 minutes of steaming, depending on the desired doneness. Beautifully steamed eggs have whites firm to the touch and creamy, nearly set golden yolks. Steamed eggs are ideal to mash into grilled toast. The satiny egg texture melts against the crisp buttered bread.

Scrambling with Ease

Scrambling eggs requires a nonstick egg pan and a wooden spoon or spatula (to keep from scratching the treated surface of the pan).

Beating the eggs is a matter of style and desired effect. For uniformly golden eggs, beat the eggs until the yolk and white are thoroughly blended. For marbled eggs that appear streaked, mix until the yolks barely break, or crack whole eggs into a warm pan and scramble over low heat until the eggs set to the desired consistency.

Blend eggs quickly; a fork or chopstick works well, keeping air bubbles to a minimum. Overbeaten eggs become tough and lose their rising power. A whisk is not necessary unless you are beating lots of eggs.

We never add water to scrambled eggs, though some cooks prefer the lighter flavor it creates, but we occasionally add cream, butter, or crème fraîche to enrich or extend the flavor of eggs.

A variety of ingredients can be added to the eggs before they cook to infuse optimum flavor—salt and pepper, sautéed vegetables, chopped herbs, grated cheese, or cooked meat.

Tender scrambled eggs require gentle cooking over low heat. Excessive heat removes moisture and makes eggs tough. For large, voluptuous curds, cook over low heat and stir occasionally in a slow circular or figure-eight motion. For smaller curds, keep the heat low and stir more often, breaking the large curds into smaller ones as they cook.

Scrambled eggs continue to cook with the residual heat in the pan, so remove the pan from the heat a few seconds before the desired texture is reached to stop the eggs from cooking.

The Quintessential Hard-Cooked Egg

Nothing is more seductive than wedges of perfect hard-cooked egg—tender whites surrounding golden yolks—nestled into a Niçoise salad, freshly chopped on marinated green beans, delicately served on a spicy arugula salad, or sprinkled over an anchovy tomato pizza. Below is an easy foolproof method for a perfect hard-cooked egg and from there, anything is possible.

Very fresh eggs are difficult to peel because the air pocket beneath the shell hasn't yet developed, which is why eggshells stick to the egg white. Eggs that are a week old are best to hard-cook. If you use very fresh eggs, add 2 teaspoons of salt to the water. The salt reacts through the porous shell, helping to separate the thin membrane from the white.

Depending on how many eggs you are cooking, bring an appropriate-size pot of water to a full boil. Place the eggs gently in the water with a Chinese strainer or a slotted spoon. Turn the heat down *slightly* to keep the vigorous boil from cracking the eggs against the pot. After exactly 8 minutes, remove the eggs swiftly. Using the strainer or slotted spoon, plunge the eggs into an ice-water bath to cool. After 1 minute, crack and peel the eggs. Place the peeled eggs in the ice bath for another minute, then remove. The yolks will be a deep golden orange—just set, perfect for pristine garnishes.

For firmer yolks, cook the eggs 9 to 10 minutes. Nine-minute eggs are ideal for sieving cleanly through a fine-mesh metal strainer over Egg and Beet Salad (page 64); 10-minute eggs are great for Nanny's Sweet Pickled Egg Salad (page 49) and Ham and Egg Croquettes (page 17).

Eggs and Bread, a Perfect Pair

Eggs cooked a variety of ways are forever complemented by the crisp texture of bread. Many of our recipes call for bread accompaniments such as toasted bread crumbs, crisp buttery croutons or bâtons, and grilled or toasted bread. These recipes are best when made with day-old, artisanally crafted loaves—coarse-crumbed, French- or Italian-style breads, slightly sour or sweet, with a crunchy crust. These kinds of breads make delicious irregularly shaped bread crumbs full of taste and crunch, croutons that soak up the pure flavor of olive oil or butter, and superior toast that is firm and slightly chewy.

We also use *pain de mie,* bread made with milk. Its rich-tasting flavor, fine-crumbed texture, and soft crust are ideal for Croque-Madame (page 62) and Nanny's Sweet Pickled Egg Salad (page 49).

Season to Taste

All the recipes in this book have been tested using kosher salt, an additive-free, mild, and clean-tasting salt. The size of the flakes gives you more control as you rub small pinches between your fingers. Kosher salt is not as strong as regular table salt and dissolves quickly into foods.

We season each element in the cooking process. For example, in the Onion and Cider Omelet (page 22), we lightly salt the onions as they caramelize to bring out the full onion flavor; we then salt the eggs to enhance their flavor. Seasoning by steps delivers fuller flavors to the finished omelet. Taste at each stage.

Country Eggs

The egg recipes in this, the first half of the book, convey all the ease, comfort, and rusticity of life in the country, where sweet-smelling breezes stir the air; time slows down, our senses awaken.

All the recipes contain straightforward cooking techniques that also mirror the country life—a simple omelet, eggs fried in fruity olive oil, egg salad oozing from between slices of bread, and crispy egg croquettes.

The recipes in "Farmhouse Eggs" pair freshly laid eggs with humble ingredients like tart apples, wild dandelion greens, and spring onions. The recipes in "Summertime Eggs" take their inspiration from the vegetable garden. "Eggs on the Go" includes simple recipes, like Gougères (page 45) and Scrambled Egg Burrito (page 53)—ideal for day trips or country jaunts.

farmhouse eggs

Apple orchards,
homemade fruit preserves,
hearth cookery,
checkered tablecloths
set the scene for these rustic recipes.
Fried eggs imbued with
nutty wild mushrooms
and preserve—laced omelets
evoke the farmhouse
wherever one may be.

APRICOT JAM OMELET

FOR EACH OMELET

Creamy layers of egg rolled over dollops of apricot jam, or your favorite fruit preserve—something from an older, slower world.

2 eggs
Salt to taste
I tablespoon unsalted butter
2 tablespoons apricot jam
Powdered sugar (optional), for garnish

Beat the eggs in a bowl and season with a little salt. Over medium-high heat, melt the butter in an omelet or nonstick pan. After the butter foams and right before it begins to brown, pour in the beaten eggs. Keep the heat medium high to quickly cook the egg mixture as it hits the pan. As the egg begins to set, pull the sides into the center slightly with a wooden spoon or single chopstick to let the raw egg run underneath. Repeat two or three times until most of the omelet is set, while the surface remains moist and creamy.

Place the apricot jam on the omelet. Tip the pan forward to force the egg to roll back onto itself. Continue rolling and gently flipping until you have rolled it completely into a little oval shape. Slide the omelet from the pan onto a plate. Allow the omelet to sit for a moment before eating. Garnish with powdered sugar.

CARAMELIZED APPLE OMELET

Tart and suave flavors harmonize in a plump omelet. For variety you can add one or two teaspoons of Calvados or rum to the apples as they cook. Try serving this with a heady stout beer.

½ apple (Gala, Sierra Beauty, Fuji, Braeburn, or Granny Smith)

1½ tablespoons unsalted butter

1 tablespoon sugar (optional)

Salt to taste

2 eggs

Powdered sugar (optional), for garnish

Peel, core, and cut the apple into slices no thinner than ⅛ inch thick.

Melt half of the butter in a nonstick or omelet pan over medium heat. Drop in the apple slices. Sauté them with a little sugar, if desired, until they are golden brown on both sides and tender to the touch. Add another teaspoon of butter if the slices look dry. Allow 15 minutes for them to become caramelized. Cover the pan to speed things up. Season with a tiny pinch of salt.

Beat the eggs and lightly season with salt. Add the remaining butter to the pan, turn the heat up to medium high, and pour the egg over the apple slices. Let the egg set on the bottom of the pan. Lift the egg up with a wooden spoon or chopstick to permit the raw egg to run underneath. When most of the egg has set and the top is moist and creamy, lift the edge of the omelet and fold it onto itself. Flip it gently to roll it closed. When the omelet is rolled up, flip it once more to get it to "seal." Roll the omelet onto a warm plate. Sprinkle with powdered sugar if serving as a dessert.

CHORIZO SCRAMBLED EGGS

FOR TWO

Chorizo is an aromatic Mexican pork sausage traditionally flavored with dried ancho and pasilla chiles, cinnamon, clove, and vinegar. Here we caramelize the sausage, then scramble it with the eggs.

1½ teaspoons canola or vegetable oil
½ cup crumbled chorizo sausage
⅓ cup diced yellow onion
4 eggs
Salt to taste
4 or more corn tortillas, warmed

In a medium nonstick pan or skillet, heat the oil and cook the chorizo over medium-low heat, stirring frequently to break up the sausage. Remove the sausage from the pan and discard most of the fat, reserving 1 tablespoon. Wipe the pan clean and add the diced onion and the reserved fat to the pan. Cook the onion until tender. Return the chorizo to the pan.

continued

Beat the eggs and season lightly with salt. Scramble the sausage and eggs together over medium heat until the eggs are just set. Slide the eggs onto warm corn tortillas on warm plates and serve with refried beans, sour cream, and radishes.

DANDELION SALAD WITH A POACHED EGG

FOR FOUR

Strong-tasting dandelion greens provide robust flavor for a poached egg. Red wine vinaigrette, garlic croutons, and bacon complete this variation on the timeless bistro salad. Use small tender dandelion greens as opposed to the mature kind, which are better for stewing.

Small loaf rustic French bread
3 tablespoons extra virgin olive oil, plus more for brushing
Salt to taste
1 teaspoon Dijon mustard
1 tablespoon red wine vinegar
Freshly ground black pepper to taste
½ pound thick-sliced bacon (optional)
¾ pound tender dandelion greens, washed and dried
4 eggs
1 garlic clove, peeled

Preheat the oven to 300°F.

Make unusual croutons by using just the crust of the bread: Shave off the top and sides. Trim 8 large bite-size pieces, 2 inches by 2 inches, and reserve the shaved loaf of bread for bread crumbs. Place the thin curved croutons on a baking sheet, drizzle the insides of the pieces with olive oil, and sprinkle with salt. Bake for 10 minutes, or until golden.

Whisk together the mustard, red wine vinegar, olive oil, salt, and pepper. Cut the bacon into 1-inch squares and brown in a frying pan. Pour off all the fat and combine the bacon with the dandelion greens in a salad bowl.

Poach the eggs in gently simmering water, about 3 minutes. Lift the eggs out with a slotted spoon and blot them gently with a towel. Trim the egg whites if necessary.

Toss the dandelions and bacon with the vinaigrette and mix thoroughly. Rub the garlic clove lightly across each toasted crouton and toss the croutons liberally into the salad to moisten lightly. Place the tossed salad on four plates and top each salad with a poached egg. Pull the croutons from the greens so you can see them. Serve immediately.

EGGS IN DUCK FAT

FOR TWO

Duck fat lends a distinctive flavor to many dishes.
In the autumn and winter months, we keep a sealed ramekin of
duck fat in our fridge for when we get the urge to fry eggs!

2 thick slices rustic French bread

Salt to taste

Freshly ground black pepper to taste

3 tablespoons plus I teaspoon duck fat

4 eggs

2 teaspoons minced shallot

I ½ teaspoons red wine vinegar

I tablespoon chopped fresh parsley or other favorite herb

Cut the bread into small croutons. Toss them with salt and pepper. Heat 1½ tablespoons of the duck fat in a cast-iron skillet and gently fry the croutons until golden brown over medium-low heat, 5 to 8 minutes. Blot on paper towels and keep warm.

In the same skillet, heat another 1½ tablespoons of duck fat. Let the fat become very hot, but not to the smoking point. Crack open 2 of the eggs into the skillet; the eggs will immediately begin to sizzle. Let the whites set, then tilt the skillet forward. Use a spoon to baste the eggs with the duck fat until the yolks begin to set, about 30 seconds. Lift the eggs out of the skillet with a spatula. Blot on paper towels.

Repeat with the other 2 eggs. Place 2 eggs each on warm plates.

To the same skillet, add the shallot, a pinch of salt, the 1 teaspoon of duck fat, and the red wine vinegar. Swirling the skillet over high heat, bring the mixture to a boil and add the parsley. Remove from the heat and spoon the shallot-parsley mixture over the warm eggs; sprinkle with the warm croutons.

HAM AND EGG CROQUETTES

FOR FOUR

These croquettes are richly textured, with soft savory centers and a crisp bread crumb coating. Serve them alone, with fresh tomato purée (page 58) as a dipping sauce, or with thickly sliced tomatoes and fresh basil or spicy watercress.

Eight 9-minute hard-cooked eggs (see page 6)
3 tablespoons unsalted butter
½ cup all-purpose flour
1⅓ cups milk
1 cup chopped cooked bacon or ham (optional)
Salt to taste
Freshly ground black pepper to taste
1½ cups fresh bread crumbs
¾ cup peanut or canola oil

continued

Peel and chop the eggs into equal-size pieces, about ¾ inch. Prepare a simple white sauce to bind the egg by first melting the butter in a small saucepan. Add the flour and whisk well. Cook for 4 to 6 minutes. Slowly whisk in the milk and cook an additional 6 to 8 minutes, or until the sauce is thickened. Mix well and cook over low heat for 5 to 10 minutes until the sauce is thick. Remove from the heat and cool.

Combine the chopped eggs, the white sauce, and, if you like, the chopped bacon or ham. Season with salt and pepper. Let the mixture cool completely. This will make forming the croquettes much easier.

Spread the bread crumbs on a plate. Form the egg mixture into small rectangular shapes no more than 1 inch thick and roll them in the bread crumbs.

Heat the oil in a cast-iron skillet to 325°F. Lightly fry the croquettes on each side for 2 minutes or more, depending on their thickness, until they are golden and crisp. Blot on paper towels and serve.

HOMEMADE MAYONNAISE

ABOUT 1 CUP

*With mayonnaise made at home, the purity of the ingredients is certain,
and you control the tartness and flavor to suit your taste.*

1 egg yolk
¼ teaspoon salt
1 teaspoon champagne vinegar
½ cup pure olive oil
½ cup canola oil
Finely ground white pepper to taste

Whisk the egg yolk, salt, and vinegar together by hand in a stainless steel
bowl or blend in a food processor or blender for 10 seconds or so. Mix
the olive oil with the canola oil. Either by hand or machine, slowly combine the oil with the egg mixture, drop by drop, to emulsify and thicken
the mixture. (An inexpensive plastic squeeze bottle is a useful tool for
making mayonnaise. You can control the drops of oil with real certainty.)
After a few tablespoons of oil have been added, begin to add the oil in a
thin steady stream. If the mayonnaise becomes too thick to whisk easily,
thin it with a few drops of water. Continue until all of the oil is combined
and the mayonnaise has thickened. Taste and adjust the seasoning with
a little additional salt, vinegar, and a pinch of white pepper.

Mayonnaise will keep for up to 3 days tightly covered and refrigerated.

MASCARPONE OMELET WITH GARDEN HERBS

FOR TWO

Fresh chervil, chives, parsley, and tarragon are the fragrant "fab four" of the herb world. Combine them with whole eggs to create an aromatic omelet enriched with sweet Italian mascarpone. Serve it with chilled glasses of Soave and a roasted wild mushroom salad. Eat beneath a plum tree, if you have one, as we do.

1 tablespoon each chopped fresh chervil, parsley, chives, and tarragon

5 eggs

Salt to taste

Freshly ground white pepper to taste

2 heaping tablespoons mascarpone

1 tablespoon unsalted butter

Chop the herbs as close to preparation time as possible. Beat the eggs lightly with a little salt and pepper and the mascarpone. The cheese should not be completely blended into the eggs. Fold in the chopped herbs.

Melt the butter in a nonstick skillet or egg pan over high heat until the butter is nearly browned but not quite. Pour in the egg mixture and cook the omelet by pulling the sides of the egg into the center several times to let the raw egg run under and set. Repeat two or three times. As the egg sets, fold the egg onto itself and begin to roll. Flip the omelet once or twice to secure the roll. Gently slice the omelet in two and slide onto two warm plates.

Mashed Potato–Baked Eggs

FOR TWO

We braise rather than boil our potatoes, then mash them. The egg
bakes in the fluffy potatoes—irresistible to children
and adults alike. As a variation, you can add chopped bacon,
ham, or chicken to the mashed potatoes.

FOR THE MASHED POTATOES

**2 large Yukon Gold potatoes, peeled and
cut into small chunks**

¾ cup water

Salt to taste

4 tablespoons unsalted butter

Freshly ground black pepper to taste

2 eggs

2 tablespoons grated Parmesan cheese

**1 tablespoon chopped fresh parsley, chives,
or other favorite herb, for garnish**

Preheat the oven to 400°F.

Combine the potatoes, water, salt, and 3 tablespoons of the butter in a saucepan over medium heat. When the butter has melted and the water has come to a boil, stir the potatoes, reduce the temperature to low, and cover tightly with a lid. After 10 minutes, check the potatoes. If the water has evaporated, add ¼ cup water and stir. Continue to cook until the potatoes are completely cooked through, about 20 minutes. After the potatoes are soft, mash well and moisten with 1 to 2 tablespoons of water if necessary and the other tablespoon of butter. Season with salt and pepper.

Place $3/4$ cup of the mashed potatoes in each of two small buttered gratin dishes or baking ramekins. Make a deep well in the center of the mashed potatoes. Crack an egg into each well and sprinkle 1 tablespoon of the grated Parmesan cheese over the top of each. Place in the oven and bake for 12 to 15 minutes, depending on how cooked you want the eggs. Garnish with the chopped herbs.

ONION AND CIDER OMELET

FOR EACH OMELET

Sweet spring onions couldn't be better than when flavored with fruity cider vinegar, then enveloped with egg.

2 tablespoons unsalted butter
$1/2$ spring onion, trimmed and sliced into thin slivers
Salt to taste
2 teaspoons apple cider vinegar
2 eggs
White Cheddar cheese (optional), for garnish

Melt 1 tablespoon of the butter over medium heat in a nonstick pan. After the butter foams, turn the heat to low and add the onion slivers. Cook until they are tender and translucent, about 10 minutes, stirring occasionally. Season the onion with salt and add the apple cider vinegar; continue to cook the onion over low heat until the vinegar is completely absorbed.

Lightly beat the eggs, season with salt, and add the softened onion. Melt the remaining 1 tablespoon of butter in the pan over medium-high heat. Brown the butter to bring out its nutty flavor. Add the egg to the hot pan. As the egg begins to set, pull the sides into the center with a wooden spoon or chopstick to let the raw egg run underneath. Repeat this two or three times over medium to high heat. Tip the pan forward to force the egg to roll onto itself. Continue rolling and gently flipping until you have rolled it into a little oval shape. Slide the omelet from the pan onto a warm plate. If desired, with a peeler, garnish the omelet with shaves of sharp Cheddar cheese.

PICKLED HERRING AND HARD-COOKED EGG

This is evocative of many family gatherings where meals begin with an
appetizer of egg, herring, and dill potatoes. Wonderful additions to the table
are rye crackers, crisp radishes, butter, and hard cheese.
Don't forget to chill the aquavit. Skoal!

FOR THE PICKLED HERRING
3 medium brined herring fillets
½ teaspoon whole allspice, lightly crushed
I bay leaf
One ½-inch piece ginger, peeled and thinly sliced
I small red onion, thinly sliced
I small carrot, peeled and sliced
½ cup white vinegar
½ cup less 2 tablespoons sugar

Three 9-minute hard-cooked eggs (see page 6)
8 small red potatoes, boiled and kept warm
I tablespoon chopped fresh chives
I tablespoon chopped fresh dill
Swedish hard bread (rye crackers)

Soak the herring overnight in cold water. Rinse well. Slice the herring
crosswise into 1-inch slices and layer with the next five ingredients in a

glass jar. Heat the vinegar and sugar together until the sugar dissolves. Chill and pour the brine over the herring. Let stand for 3 days sealed tightly in the refrigerator.

Before your guests arrive, peel the eggs and slice them across the center. Arrange the egg slices on a long serving dish and sprinkle with chives. Place the warm potatoes sprinkled with dill on the serving dish. Serve the herring from the marinating jar. Pass the Swedish hard bread. Each person can make a small plate of herring and egg to eat together with rye crackers and warm potatoes.

WATERCRESS EGG SALSA

ABOUT 1 ¹/₂ CUPS

A refreshing sauce for poached or grilled fish, roasted meat, roasted or raw vegetables, or just grilled bread. Finely chopped capers, anchovies, and cornichons, added with discretion, are great accompaniments.

Two 8-minute hard-cooked eggs (see page 6)
1 bunch watercress
¼ cup or more extra virgin olive oil
**½ cup finely chopped sweet onion
(Maui, Vidalia, or Walla Walla)**

Salt to taste
Freshly ground black pepper to taste
1 teaspoon red wine vinegar (optional)

continued

Peel and finely chop the eggs. Rinse the watercress under cold water and dry in a salad spinner. Discard any imperfect leaves and roughly chop the greens with a sharp knife, keeping a little of the stems. Combine the chopped egg with the watercress. Add the olive oil and onion. Season with salt and pepper. Flavor with the red wine vinegar, if desired.

Adjust the seasoning and consistency to taste. The consistency should be that of salsa. Make it thinner by adding a bit more olive oil or thicker by adding a bit more onion or watercress.

The salsa will keep 2 days tightly covered and refrigerated.

WILD MUSHROOMS "SUNNY-SIDE UP"

FOR TWO

Sliced wild mushrooms set into the egg whites like a mosaic.

**2½ tablespoons duck fat, pure olive oil, or
unsalted butter (or more if needed)**

**2 cups cleaned, sliced wild mushrooms
(chanterelles, cèpes, shiitakes, or a combination)**

Salt to taste

1 tablespoon chopped fresh parsley

1 teaspoon finely chopped garlic

4 eggs

Freshly ground black pepper to taste

4 slices rustic bread, lightly toasted or grilled

Melt the duck fat in a cast-iron skillet over medium heat. Sauté the mushrooms until they are tender and golden, about 10 minutes, depending on their moisture content. The mushrooms are cooked when they are tender to the touch and have reabsorbed the moisture they initially expelled. Season the mushrooms with salt. Remove half of the mushrooms from the skillet and set aside.

Mix the chopped parsley and garlic together.

Over medium-high heat, spread out the mushrooms in the skillet, crack open 2 eggs over the mushrooms, and cook sunny-side up. Using a spoon, baste the egg yolks with hot oil gathered by tilting the skillet forward. When the mushrooms are completely set into the whites, lift out the eggs as one mass onto a warm plate. Quickly repeat for the other serving, using the set-aside mushrooms. Add another $\frac{1}{2}$ teaspoon of fat if necessary. Serve the eggs with a generous sprinkling of the parsley-garlic mixture and pepper and pieces of warm toast.

summertime eggs

Juicy tomatoes,
sweet crisp peppers,
and fragrant basil
inspire this group of recipes,
which capture the season
with its
sun-soaked days
and its
sensual bounty.

AUNTIE BELL'S SCRAMBLED EGGS

*Sweet-smelling juicy tomatoes that are perfectly ripe, at their
peak of sweetness, melt in olive oil in a moment, permeating
scrambled eggs with unsurpassable aroma and flavor.
We choose varieties of heirloom tomatoes for their vibrant color
contrast against the yellow hue of the eggs.*

FOR THE BREAD CRUMBS
Several slices day-old French bread
1 tablespoon pure olive oil
Salt to taste

3 tablespoons pure olive oil
1 pound ripe summer tomatoes, coarsely chopped
Salt to taste
8 fresh basil leaves
10 eggs
Freshly ground white pepper to taste

Preheat the oven to 300°F.

Remove the crusts from the bread and cut the bread into chunks.
Place in a food processor and process until roughly the size of peas.
Drizzle with olive oil and sprinkle with salt. Bake for 10 to 15 minutes,
until golden and crisp. Keep the bread crumbs warm.

continued

Put the olive oil in a 10- or 12-inch nonstick pan over medium heat. Add the tomatoes and season with salt. Cook for 5 minutes, or until slightly softened but not puréed. Add torn basil leaves so the perfume starts to release.

Beat the eggs lightly and season with salt and white pepper. Combine with the tomatoes and, over medium-low heat, gently scramble the eggs. Garnish with warm crisp bread crumbs.

BASIL AÏOLI

A LITTLE OVER I CUP

We love this summer variation on basic aïoli. The basil flavor is a fragrant surprise for sandwiches, grilled fish, and vegetables.

I egg yolk
I teaspoon water
Salt to taste
I ¼ cups pure olive oil
I small garlic clove, peeled
20 fresh basil leaves, roughly chopped

Whisk together the egg yolk, water, and a pinch of salt by hand in a stainless steel bowl or blend in a food processor or blender. Blend for 10 seconds or so. Either by hand, whisking constantly, or in a machine, slowly combine the olive oil with the egg mixture, drop by drop, to emulsify and thicken the mixture. (An inexpensive plastic squeeze bottle is a useful tool for making mayonnaise. You can control the drops of oil with real certainty.) After a few tablespoons of oil have been added, and the sauce has started to thicken, begin to add the oil in a thin steady stream. If the mayonnaise becomes too thick to whisk easily, thin it with a few drops of water. Continue until all of the oil is combined and the mayonnaise has thickened.

A mortar with a pestle is the best way to purée a small amount of garlic and basil. Grind the garlic clove with a little salt until it is puréed. Add the basil and grind with a sprinkling of salt until the basil and garlic become a relatively smooth paste.

Add 1 heaping tablespoon of basil-garlic purée to the mayonnaise and blend well, until thoroughly mixed. Taste and adjust the seasoning if necessary. If the sauce is too thick, add 1 teaspoon of water.

Basil aïoli is best when you let it rest for an hour or so, covered, in the refrigerator to let the flavors marry. It will keep up to 2 days, covered and refrigerated.

EGGS IN A TOMATO NEST

FOR FOUR

Prepare these charming nests ahead of time. When the guests arrive,
bake the tomatoes in a hot oven, then serve them with a basket of grilled or
toasted bread rubbed lightly with a garlic clove.

½ cup fresh bread crumbs
2 teaspoons plus 2 tablespoons extra virgin olive oil
Salt to taste
4 medium vine-ripened tomatoes
4 eggs
Freshly ground black pepper to taste
2 teaspoons chopped fresh tarragon
2 teaspoons chopped fresh chervil
1 tablespoon minced shallot
2 teaspoons unsalted butter
½ pound garden lettuces
1 tablespoon balsamic vinegar

Preheat the oven to 400°F.

Toss the bread crumbs with the 2 teaspoons of olive oil and a pinch of salt. Place on a baking sheet in the hot oven for 5 or 6 minutes to dry them out. Do not brown. Remove from the oven and set aside.

Rinse and dry off the tomatoes. Insert a sharp paring knife into the top of each tomato and cut out a 2-inch-diameter section. Gently remove the pulp and seeds with a spoon to create a little cup. Season the tomatoes liberally with salt. Crack an egg into each tomato. Season the eggs with salt and pepper. Put the tomatoes on a small sheet pan or in a shallow baking dish and place them in the hot oven for 10 minutes.

Combine the tarragon, chervil, and shallot with the bread crumbs while the tomatoes are baking. After 10 minutes, sprinkle the bread crumb mixture and ½ teaspoon of the butter over the top of each egg. Continue to bake for 6 more minutes, or until the crumbs are golden and the eggs are just set.

Dress the garden lettuces with the 2 tablespoons of oil and the vinegar and place on four salad plates. Remove the tomatoes with a spatula and nestle them into the lettuce.

HUEVOS À LA FLAMENCO

FOR FOUR

Use a cazuela, *a Spanish earthenware cooking pan, to cook
the onion, tomato, and bell peppers on the stove; add eggs, then finish in the
oven. The finished dish rises into a golden dome speckled with colors
that reflect the Spanish flag.*

3 tablespoons pure olive oil
2 garlic cloves, peeled and crushed
¾ cup diced yellow onion
¼ pound andouille or chorizo sausage
½ cup green bean pieces (1 inch)
Salt to taste
1½ cups thinly sliced roasted red bell pepper
1½ cups peeled, seeded, and diced tomato
1 tablespoon cooking sherry
8 eggs
¼ teaspoon Spanish ground red pepper or cayenne pepper

Preheat the oven to 350°F.

Heat a *cazuela* on the stove over medium heat (use a large sauté pan
if you don't have a *cazuela*). Add the olive oil, garlic, and onion and
cook covered over low heat until the onion is tender, stirring occasionally. Thinly slice the andouille or chorizo sausage into coin shapes and
add to the onion. Add the green beans, season liberally with salt, and

continue to stir occasionally. Combine the roasted pepper with the tomato and the cooking sherry. Add to the pan and simmer together for 5 to 8 minutes until all the flavors of the sauce marry.

Lightly beat the eggs and season with salt and hot pepper. Pour the eggs into the vegetable-sausage mixture, place the pan in the oven, and bake until the eggs are firm to the touch, about 20 minutes, depending on the thickness of the cooking vessel and your oven. (If you are not using a *cazuela*, use a deep standard baking dish to finish the eggs in the oven.) Insert a knife into the center; if the center isn't runny, the eggs are done.

MACARONI AND EGG SALAD

FOR FOUR

Crumbles of hard-cooked egg and freshly ground nutmeg endow this basic macaroni salad with subtle richness. Nutmeg adds a vital, earthy flavor, an important counterpoint to the other components. For a variation, you can use less mayonnaise and substitute a fruity olive oil, then season accordingly with more lemon, salt, black pepper, and nutmeg.

1½ cups dried macaroni or other pasta

2 teaspoons or more salt

Three 9-minute hard-cooked eggs (see page 6)

½ cup Homemade Mayonnaise (page 19)

3 tablespoons chopped fresh parsley

Juice of half a lemon

Freshly ground black pepper to taste

½ teaspoon freshly grated nutmeg

½ cup chopped roasted red bell pepper or pimiento (optional)

Cook the pasta in boiling water for about 6 minutes. Drain and rinse, drizzle with a little olive oil, and salt to taste. Allow to cool.

Rinse, peel, and let the 9-minute hard-cooked eggs cool.

Dress the pasta with the mayonnaise, half the chopped parsley, lemon juice, salt, pepper, and nutmeg and mix well. For added bright color, add the bell pepper. Taste and adjust the seasoning.

Put the eggs through a sieve or finely hand chop. Serve the macaroni salad in a bowl; garnish with all of the egg and sprinkle with the remaining chopped parsley.

Pesto Scrambled Eggs

FOR FOUR

*Use a mortar and pestle to turn basil into
authentic pesto and drizzle
the pesto over corn-studded scrambled eggs.*

FOR THE PESTO
1 small garlic clove, peeled
2 cups fresh basil leaves, roughly chopped
⅓ cup extra virgin olive oil
Salt to taste
¼ cup pine nuts
¼ cup freshly grated Parmesan cheese

8 slices rustic French bread
2 ears fresh shucked corn
2 tablespoons unsalted butter
8 eggs
Salt to taste

continued

Grind the garlic in a mortar to make a rough paste. Add some of the basil, a drizzle of the oil—just enough to moisten the leaves—and a tiny pinch of salt to create a pulpy mass. Grind in some of the pine nuts until most are broken down, then repeat the process adding more basil, oil, and pine nuts until all the ingredients are incorporated into a smooth paste. Add the grated cheese and taste for salt, adding a little more if necessary. The pesto should glisten with olive oil around the edges. Let the pesto rest for an hour or more for the flavors to marry.

Toast or grill the bread slices and warm four plates.

Remove the corn kernels from the cob by running a sharp knife down the sides over a bowl to collect the kernels. Melt the butter in a medium-size nonstick pan over medium heat. Add the corn and sauté for 1 to 2 minutes. Beat the eggs and season with salt. Reduce the heat to low and pour the eggs into the pan with the corn. Scramble to the desired doneness. Taste for salt and spoon the eggs onto the warm plates, topping each with 2 tablespoons of pesto and serving each with 2 pieces of bread.

Pipérade

The Basque specialty of sautéed bell peppers, tomatoes, and garlic is the epitome of late-summer flavor, made richer with the addition of fluffy eggs. Serve this with a small garden salad dressed with your favorite oil and vinegar.

2 medium red bell peppers, cored and seeded
1 medium green bell pepper, cored and seeded
6 tablespoons pure olive oil
2 small garlic cloves, peeled and crushed
Salt to taste
Freshly ground black pepper to taste
2 pounds ripe tomatoes, peeled, seeded, and chopped
¼ teaspoon chile flakes
20 slices (⅜ inch thick) baguette
7 eggs
8 to 10 fresh basil leaves, for garnish
4 slices ham or prosciutto, grilled

Remove the membranes from the peppers. Slice the peppers into thin strips. Heat 4 tablespoons of the olive oil in a skillet and sauté the peppers with the garlic. Season with salt and pepper. Cover and cook until tender, about 15 minutes, stirring occasionally. Add the tomatoes and chile flakes and cook until soft and thick, about 30 minutes.

continued

Meanwhile, in a cast-iron skillet, heat the remaining 2 tablespoons of olive oil over medium heat and fry the baguette slices, in batches, until golden on both sides, about 5 minutes. Keep the croutons warm.

Lightly beat the eggs and season with salt. Add the beaten eggs to the vegetable mixture and stir from the edges inward over low heat for 3 minutes, or until the mixture has thickened and the eggs and vegetables become creamy. (If the heat is too high, the eggs may form clumps.) Taste for salt and adjust.

Spoon the eggs into four warm bowls and garnish with hand-torn basil leaves. Add the croutons and a slice of ham or prosciutto to each.

SORREL OMELET

FOR EACH OMELET

The lemony flavor of tender sorrel leaves complements eggs with a mild tartness. We use duck fat for sweetness, as is done in the Southwest of France. Serve with french fries and a glass of lightly chilled chardonnay.

10 to 12 fresh sorrel leaves
3 eggs, beaten
Salt to taste
Freshly ground white pepper to taste
1 tablespoon duck fat or unsalted butter

Wash the sorrel leaves under cold water and dry in a salad spinner or pat dry. Remove the stems. Slice the leaves in 1-inch-wide diagonal pieces. In a small bowl, combine the sorrel and eggs with a little salt and a twist of white pepper.

Over medium-high heat, melt the duck fat or butter in a small 7- or 8-inch nonstick egg pan. When the fat is hot but before it smokes, add the egg-sorrel mixture. Let the first layer of egg set on the bottom and the sides. Keep the heat medium high and pull the sides of the setting egg into the center a few times to let the uncooked egg run underneath and set. As soon as most of the egg begins to set and the top is creamy and moist, roll the omelet by tilting the pan forward and let the edges roll over. Reduce the heat to medium and gently flip the omelet once or twice to finish cooking the inside of the omelet. Roll onto a warm plate and eat immediately.

Squash Blossom and Zucchini Frittata

FOR TWO

Visit your local farmers' market to find squash blossoms at their absolute peak. Finish the zucchini-and-squash-blossom-studded eggs in the oven to allow the frittata to rise. Serve with a chilled glass of rosé.

5 or 6 medium squash blossoms

1 medium green zucchini

1 tablespoon unsalted butter or pure olive oil

Salt to taste

3 eggs

Fresh basil leaves, for garnish

1 tablespoon freshly grated Parmesan cheese (optional), for garnish

Preheat the oven to 350°F.

Trim the stems of the squash blossoms up to the base of the flowers. Cut the blossoms diagonally into ½-inch bands. Rinse and slice off the tips of the zucchini. Cut the zucchini into long thin matchstick shapes (it should yield just under 1 cup of matchsticks). Over medium heat, melt the butter or olive oil in an ovenproof nonstick skillet. Sauté the zucchini lightly for 1 minute, then add the squash blossoms, toss together, and season with salt.

Beat the eggs in a bowl, season lightly with salt, and add to the squash blossoms and zucchini in the pan. Turn the heat to low and stir for 1 minute. Place on the middle rack in the oven for 7 to 8 minutes, or until the frittata has set and gently risen. Allow the frittata to rest for 1 minute, then carefully slide it onto a warm plate. Garnish with a few torn basil leaves and, if desired, sprinkle Parmesan cheese on top.

eggs on the go

Seaside strolls, forest picnics,
and garden lunches are just a few
plein air destinations to relish savory
appetizers and sandwiches.
Innovative twists to the
familiar, such as Green Pepper
"Fried" Egg Sandwich (page 48),
make the notion of
sandwiches irresistible
once more.

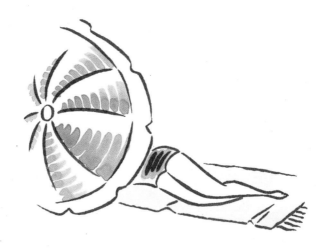

Gougères

*These golden, savory, Gruyère-laced puffs are delicious served either warm
with red wine or cold with white wine. Once cooled, they make excellent
snacks for hikes and picnics.*

3 tablespoons unsalted butter
½ cup water
1 scant cup all-purpose flour
3 eggs
1⅓ cups grated Gruyère cheese
½ teaspoon or more salt
⅔ cup roughly chopped bacon (optional)

Combine the butter and water in a small saucepan and bring to a boil.
Add the flour all at once, quickly stirring with a wooden spoon until the
batter is smooth and detaches from the sides of the saucepan. The
dough will form a ball around the spoon. (This process moves pretty
quickly.)

Remove the pan from the heat and beat in the eggs, one at a time,
until each egg has been thoroughly incorporated into the dough. Stir in
the cheese, add the salt to taste, and, if you like, the bacon. Let the
dough rest for an hour.

Preheat the oven to 375°F.

On a cookie sheet lined with parchment paper, use two spoons to form 2-inch balls with peaks. Bake for 25 minutes, or until the blade of a knife when stuck into the center comes out clean. The gougères will puff to twice their size and turn golden brown.

GRATINÉED DEVILED EGGS

FOR SIX TO EIGHT

The allure of this charming recipe lies in a quick pass under the broiler to gratinée. We serve little antipasto plates of olives, roasted peppers, salami, pickles, and bread to accompany these pretty eggs.

Eight 9-minute hard-cooked eggs (see page 6)
2 tablespoons Dijon mustard
3 tablespoons heavy cream
2 tablespoons minced shallot
1 tablespoon white wine vinegar, plus a little extra
1 tablespoon chopped fresh chives
1 tablespoon chopped fresh tarragon
Salt to taste
Freshly ground white pepper to taste
Soft unsalted butter

Preheat the broiler.

Peel the eggs and slice them in half lengthwise. Remove the yolks and place in a small mixing bowl. Blend the yolks with the mustard, cream, shallot, vinegar, chives, tarragon, salt, and white pepper. Place the yolk mixture in a piping bag and pipe into the whites, or use a spoon to fill the egg whites with the mixture. The stuffing should sit high and fluffy on the egg whites.

Place the stuffed eggs in a baking dish or on a baking sheet and dot each egg with a little softened butter and a drop of vinegar. Broil the egg halves until the tops are lightly golden and gratinéed, 4 to 7 minutes. This is a fairly fast procedure; keep a close eye on the eggs or they may burn. Remove the eggs from the broiler and serve at once.

GREEN PEPPER "FRIED" EGG SANDWICH

FOR TWO

Suave creamy eggs meet spicy green peppers in this luscious sandwich.

2 medium green bell peppers
3 tablespoons pure olive oil
I garlic clove, peeled and crushed
¼ teaspoon chile flakes
Salt to taste
4 slices rustic French bread
2 eggs

Rinse the peppers under cold water and cut the flesh into finger shapes, approximately ½ inch thick. Trim off the interior white membranes with a sharp paring knife and eliminate the seeds and stems. In a small sauté pan, heat the olive oil with the garlic and chile flakes. When the oil is hot, add the peppers, season with salt, and sauté vigorously over medium heat until the peppers are soft and caramelized.

Lightly toast or grill the bread. Place the toasted bread on a plate.

When the peppers are tender, discard the garlic and place the peppers on 2 of the slices of bread. The peppers will moisten and flavor the bread. While the pan is still warm, into the remaining peppery oil, crack open the eggs. Season with salt and use a single chopstick to scramble the eggs quickly. Place the warm marbled eggs on the peppers and top each with a slice of toasted bread. Eat the sandwiches warm.

NANNY'S SWEET PICKLED EGG SALAD

ABOUT 1 1/2 CUPS

*Nanny's egg salad secret was the addition of finely diced sweet pickles
and a bit of the pickling juice. The eggs should be very finely chopped and
the bread should be good-quality white. (Hold the lettuce.)*

Six 10-minute hard-cooked eggs (see page 6)
1/3 cup finely diced sweet onion
1/4 cup diced sweet pickle
2 tablespoons or more pickling juice
1/4 cup Homemade Mayonnaise (page 19)
2 tablespoons chopped fresh parsley
Salt to taste
1/2 loaf (6 to 8 slices) good-quality white bread,
such as *pain de mie*

Peel and finely dice the eggs (approximately 1/4 inch thick); place in a
mixing bowl. Add the onion and pickle. Mix in 2 tablespoons of the
pickling juice and the mayonnaise. Sprinkle in the parsley and blend
the ingredients together until well mixed. Season with salt.

For every sandwich, spread 2 slices of bread with a little extra mayonnaise, place a goodly portion of egg salad on 1 slice, then cover it
with the other. Following tradition, the sandwiches should be a little
tricky to eat. Serve with salted potato chips.

POTATO EGG TORTA

FOR FOUR

This Spanish omelet is a thick egg and potato cake baked gently in the oven. You can serve it warm with toasted almonds and marinated olives, or cold, sliced and tucked between crusty bread as a sandwich.

1½ pounds Yukon Gold or Yellow Finnish potatoes
1½ teaspoons salt plus more to taste
7 eggs
1 tablespoon pure olive oil

Preheat the oven to 350°F.

Peel the potatoes and cut them into pieces approximately 1½ by 1½ inches. This will yield 2 cups of potatoes. Bring 3 quarts of water to boil with the 1½ teaspoons salt. Add the potatoes and simmer until they are tender but still intact, about 15 minutes. Drain and allow the potato pieces to completely cool on a cookie sheet.

In a large bowl, beat the eggs, season with salt, and carefully mix in the potatoes. Heat the olive oil in an ovenproof 8-inch nonstick egg pan. Combine the potato-egg mixture and cook over low heat, stirring, for 2 minutes. The stirring and gentle heat will start the cooking process. Place the pan on the center rack of the oven and bake until the *torta* has just set, 15 to 20 minutes. You can test for doneness by examining and touching the surface. If there is any runny egg in the center, return the *torta* to the oven for a few more minutes.

Once the *torta* is cooked, let it rest for a few minutes, then invert it onto a plate. Allow the *torta* to set, then slice it into small wedges and serve.

STEAMED MUSSELS AND FENNEL FRITTATA

FOR TWO TO FOUR

This fennel-scented frittata, laced with briny mussels, is
a perfect snack to serve in the garden or pack for a picnic at the beach.
Serve it with crusty French bread.

10 mussels
¼ cup white wine
1 thyme branch
½ cup diced yellow onion
½ cup diced fresh fennel
1½ tablespoons extra virgin olive oil, plus more for drizzling
4 eggs
Salt to taste
1 teaspoon chopped fennel fronds

Preheat the oven to 350°F.

Rinse the mussels and remove the beards with your fingers. Steam the mussels in a covered pan with 3 tablespoons of the white wine and the thyme branch for 1 to 2 minutes, or until the shells pop open.

continued

Remove the mussels from the shells. Moisten the mussels with 2 teaspoons of the cooking broth and set aside.

In a skillet, sauté the onion and diced fennel in the olive oil until tender and translucent. Add the remaining 1 tablespoon of white wine and let it evaporate.

Beat the eggs, season with salt, and add the fennel fronds. Add the eggs to the onion-fennel mixture and sprinkle in the mussels. Cook over medium-low heat for 1 to 2 minutes. Place in the oven for 8 minutes, or until the egg is just set. Remove from the oven and drizzle extra virgin olive oil over the top. Slice and serve.

SCRAMBLED EGG BURRITO

FOR FOUR TO SIX

This campfire recipe was inspired by family camping trips. (It takes a brave hiker to bear a precious dozen in his pack.) Flour tortillas steam as they act as a pan lid on top of the campfire eggs.

2 tablespoons unsalted butter or pure olive oil
1 small yellow onion, slivered
3 medium tomatoes, seeded and diced
Salt to taste
12 eggs
Four to six 8-inch flour tortillas

In a hot skillet, over your portable camping stove, heat the butter or olive oil. Add the onion to the skillet and sauté until tender. (Or gauge how much stove fuel you can spare!) Add the tomatoes to the skillet and gently cook with the onion. Season with salt. Beat the eggs with a fork and season with salt. Add the eggs to the skillet.

Make a lid for the eggs by using the tortillas: Layer 1 tortilla per person over the egg in the skillet; this helps to steam the eggs and softens the tortillas. Rotate the tortillas as necessary and stir the eggs until the desired consistency is achieved.

Scoop the eggs that haven't stuck to the skillet into the steamed tortillas. Fold the two side edges over the eggs slightly and roll up the bottom into a secure package, which makes them convenient to hold and eat.

City Eggs

These slightly soigné recipes are a bit more urbane and sophisticated than their country cousins. "Uptown Eggs" are pure theater, while "Egg a Day" offers morning eggs for city folks in a rush.

"Weekend Eggs" take you lazily through brunch and lunch, while "Eggs for Supper" segue into the evening meal and give proof to the fact that if you have half a dozen eggs in the refrigerator, a great little meal is at hand. Of course, you can always skip dinner and go straight to dessert. Check out "The After-Dinner Egg" for a chocolate soufflé, crisp fritters, and lush sabayon.

uptown eggs

"Dressed up" with
caviar, black truffles,
or smoked salmon,
and poached for a custard
or baked for a soufflé,
these uptown eggs are
"puttin' on the Ritz."

BALSAMIC FRIED EGGS

FOR ONE

*This recipe combines velvety sweet-sour balsamic vinegar with
farm-fresh eggs fried over easy in fruity olive oil.*

2 tablespoons good-quality extra virgin olive oil
2 eggs
1 ½ tablespoons aged balsamic vinegar
**Spicy lettuce (red mustard greens,
watercress, or arugula), for garnish**

In a nonstick or seasoned egg pan, heat the olive oil over medium heat.
When the oil is hot but not quite at the smoking point, crack open the
eggs into the pan and cook for about 25 seconds, keeping the heat
medium. As they puff up, baste the top of the yolks with the hot oil to
help them cook.

After the eggs set, slide them onto a warm plate. Pour off any excess
oil. Add the balsamic vinegar to the pan and let it sizzle and reduce
slightly for a moment or two. Drizzle the vinegar over the eggs and drop
a small handful of spicy garden lettuce on top. Serve with toasted bread.

BREAD CRUMB FRIED EGGS

FOR TWO

The sensation of eating poached eggs coated with bread crumbs, lightly fried,
then served with a smooth tomato sauce is addictive and worth every step!

FOR THE TOMATO SAUCE
¼ cup pure olive oil
½ cup diced yellow onion
Salt to taste
1¾ cups peeled and diced tomatoes
2 thyme branches
1 bay leaf

5 eggs
1 tablespoon water
1½ cups fresh bread crumbs
1½ cups peanut or olive oil
Salt to taste
Freshly ground black pepper to taste
Handful of arugula leaves,
roughly chopped, for garnish

Heat the ¼ cup of olive oil in a skillet and add the diced onion. Cook together over medium-low heat until the onion is tender and translucent. Season with salt. Add the tomatoes and simmer with the thyme branches and bay leaf for 10 to 15 minutes. Season with salt and remove the bay leaf and thyme branches. Purée the sauce in a food processor or food mill until it is very smooth. If the sauce is too thick to pour, thin it with a little warm water and olive oil until the desired consistency is reached. Keep it warm.

Poach 4 of the eggs in gently simmering water until just set, about 3 minutes. Lift the eggs out and blot them with a towel. Let cool and trim the edges of the whites with a paring knife for easier handling. (This may all be done several hours ahead of time.)

Whip the remaining egg in a shallow bowl and add the water. Roll the cooled poached eggs in the egg mixture, then in the bread crumbs with a slotted spoon, handling them gently. Let set for 10 minutes. In a deep-sided medium sauté pan, heat the $1\frac{1}{2}$ cups of peanut oil to 325°F. Add the breaded eggs and lightly fry each side, about 30 seconds per side, until the coating is golden and the eggs are heated through. Lift the eggs out of the oil and blot on paper towels. Warm two plates and pour $\frac{1}{4}$ cup of warm tomato sauce onto each plate. Place the eggs on the plates and season the eggs with salt and pepper. Sprinkle with arugula leaves.

CAVIAR AND SCRAMBLED EGGS IN THE SHELL

FOR FOUR

Araucana spotted chickens produce delicious-tasting eggs with
splendid blue-green shells, ideal for this precious presentation.

4 eggs, Araucana variety if possible
2 tablespoons unsalted butter
¼ cup fruity white wine
I tablespoon crème fraîche
Salt to taste
I tablespoon finely chopped fresh chives
2 ounces or more fresh caviar from a reputable source

Remove the smaller end of the eggs with a serrated knife: Cut ¾ inch
from the top, gently sawing back and forth. Reserve the tops. Empty the
eggs into a bowl. Place the shells and tops in gently boiling water for
several minutes to remove any of the white left in the shells. Drain.

Melt the butter over low heat in a nonstick egg pan. Add the white
wine and reduce by half. Whip the eggs with crème fraîche and season
lightly with salt. Add the eggs to the wine-butter reduction and gently
scramble to desired consistency over low heat to keep the eggs creamy
and tender. Sprinkle in the chives.

Fill each eggshell with the scrambled eggs. Set the filled shells into
four eggcups. Place ½ ounce of fresh caviar on each egg and place the
egg tops back on. Serve with small spoons or caviar spoons.

CHEESE SOUFFLÉ

FOR TWO TO FOUR

There isn't a more alluring dish than an airy soufflé coming out of the oven. Serve with a freshly picked salad or as an accompaniment to roasted meat.

5 tablespoons unsalted butter
5 tablespoons all-purpose flour
1 ½ cups milk
1 cup heavy cream
5 eggs, separated
6 ounces Gruyère cheese, grated
⅛ teaspoon cream of tartar (optional)

Preheat the oven to 350°F.

Melt the butter in a heavy-duty 2- to 4-quart pot. Stir in the flour and cook over low heat so the flour loses its raw taste, about 8 minutes. Remove from the heat. Combine the milk and cream and slowly pour it into the roux (flour mixture) with a whisk until it is fully blended. Simmer over very low heat for 10 minutes, or until the mixture thickens, stirring occasionally.

Place the egg yolks into a stainless steel bowl. Strain the mixture through a fine sieve into the bowl with the yolks. Whisk until well blended. Add the grated cheese and heat it gently over a saucepan of hot water over very low heat, stirring until the cheese is melted.

continued

Place the egg whites in a copper bowl and whip until stiff peaks form. If you do not have a copper bowl, combine the cream of tartar with the whites before beating. With a wide spatula, fold the whites carefully into the yolk mixture. Do not deflate the whites by stirring too much.

Butter and flour an 8-inch-diameter soufflé dish. Pour the batter into the dish (the dish will be three-quarters full) and place into the hot oven. Bake for 40 to 45 minutes. The soufflé will double in size and the top should be a deep golden color.

CROQUE-MADAME

FOR TWO

Croque-Madame, the toasted sandwich of Gruyère and ham, is distinguished from Croque-Monsieur by an egg crown. This is our version of the renowned Paris bistro snack. Serve it with cornichons and an ice-cold beer.

2½ tablespoons soft unsalted butter

½ teaspoon Dijon mustard

¼ teaspoon Worcestershire sauce

**4 thin slices *pain de mie,* or other high-quality
white bread, crusts removed**

4 thin slices Gruyère cheese

2 thin slices country-style cured ham

2 eggs

Set the oven to broil.

Mix together 1½ tablespoons of the butter, the mustard, and Worcestershire sauce. Spread the mixture on one side of 2 pieces of bread. Lay a slice of cheese, a ham slice, then another cheese slice on top. Top each with another piece of bread and press down.

In a large cast-iron skillet, melt the remaining tablespoon of butter over medium heat. When the butter is hot but not browned, place the sandwiches into the skillet and cook over low heat for 2 to 3 minutes. Cover the skillet to help the cheese melt. Turn the sandwiches over and continue to cook the other side until crisp and golden. Add a little more butter to the skillet if necessary.

Crack an egg onto each toasted sandwich and place the skillet under the broiler. Cook the eggs until they are set. Egg will run over the edges a bit. Use a spatula to place the sandwiches on plates.

EGG AND BEET SALAD

FOR FOUR

The different-colored beets and the
vibrant egg on the delicate greens evoke the sense
of spring. Serve as a first course or a light lunch.

I pound small varietal beets (Chioggia, red, and gold)
2 teaspoons minced shallot
I tablespoon champagne vinegar
I tablespoon fresh orange juice
½ teaspoon sugar
½ teaspoon salt
¼ cup extra virgin olive oil
2 eggs
½ pound lettuce (mâche, frisée, or watercress)

Preheat the oven to 375°F.

Bake the red beets in a separate pan or they will stain the other beets red. Remove the tops, rinse clean, and bake the beets in a covered pan with ½ inch water to help steam them. Bake for 1 hour, depending on their size, or until the flesh can be pierced with a knife. Let cool and peel. The skins should slip off. Cut the beets into small wedges. Keep the different colors separate. Sprinkle the beets with a little vinegar, olive oil to taste, and a pinch of salt and marinate lightly.

Prepare a vinaigrette by combining the shallot with the vinegar, orange juice, sugar, and $\frac{1}{2}$ teaspoon of salt. Let stand for 10 minutes. Whisk in the $\frac{1}{4}$ cup olive oil.

Boil the eggs for 9 minutes (see page 6) while you wash, rinse, and dry the lettuce. Peel the eggs.

Dress the greens with the vinaigrette. Place small handfuls of salad on four plates. Nestle 8 to 10 beet wedges into each salad. Sieve the eggs evenly over the salads to coat with equal parts of yolk and white.

JAPANESE SAVORY CUSTARD

FOR FOUR

Ginger-infused egg and simple broth
steam into a silky, restorative custard
as a first course or light meal.

2$\frac{1}{2}$ cups clear chicken, fish, or vegetable stock
1 tablespoon light soy sauce
1 teaspoon mirin or cooking sake
$\frac{1}{2}$ teaspoon salt
3 eggs
1 small knob of ginger, peeled and finely julienned
8 small shrimps, peeled and deveined (optional)

Set up a steamer basket in a large pot with a lid. Season the stock with the soy sauce, mirin or sake, and salt. Beat the eggs in a medium mixing bowl until lightly blended. Add the seasoned stock. Strain the mixture through a fine sieve. Add the slivered ginger.

Place 2 shrimps each into four porcelain cups and pour in the egg-broth mixture. (Each cup should hold about ¼ cup of broth.) Cover each cup with a small square of foil. Place the cups into the steamer, cover, and steam over high heat for 5 minutes. Reduce the heat to a low simmer and cook for 10 to 12 minutes. To test for doneness, insert a skewer into the custard. The egg should be delicately set and the broth should run clear around the puncture. Place the cups on small plates and serve.

SMOKED SALMON, EGG, AND ASPARAGUS SANDWICH

FOR TWO

Thinly sliced smoked salmon, lemony asparagus, and fluffy eggs combine in glorious afternoon tea sandwiches.

½ pound asparagus, ends removed and skin peeled
1 tablespoon lemon juice, preferably Meyer
1 teaspoon minced shallot
½ teaspoon salt plus more to taste
3 tablespoons pure olive oil
4 slices *pain de mie*
1 tablespoon unsalted butter
3 eggs
2 thin slices smoked salmon
1 tablespoon fresh chervil

Blanch the asparagus in rapidly boiling, lightly salted water until it is cooked through but firm, 1 to 2 minutes, depending on the thickness. Let the asparagus drain. Spread on a baking sheet to cool and finish cooking. Slice each spear lengthwise in half with a sharp paring knife.

Combine the lemon juice, shallot, and ½ teaspoon of salt. Let the shallot "marinate" for 10 minutes. Whisk in the olive oil. Adjust the seasoning.

Lightly toast or grill the bread.

continued

In a 7- or 8-inch nonstick or seasoned egg pan, melt the butter. Add the eggs and a little salt and mix well. Scramble the eggs until fluffy.

Toss the asparagus spears with the vinaigrette in a small bowl and season with salt.

Prepare the sandwiches by layering the marinated asparagus on the bottom of 2 pieces of bread and spooning the warm eggs over the asparagus. Place a slice of smoked salmon over the eggs. Sprinkle chervil over the salmon. Top each with a piece of bread or serve open-face style.

SLOW-COOKED EGGS WITH BLACK TRUFFLES

FOR FOUR

These gently scrambled eggs are laced with fresh black truffles and thickened with butter. So that the aroma of the truffle will permeate the eggs, refrigerate the eggs and truffle together in a sealed container a day before you use them.

8 eggs
Salt to taste
1 fresh black truffle
2 tablespoons soft unsalted butter
10 tablespoons cold unsalted butter
20 thin slices rustic French bread

Beat the eggs until well mixed and season with salt. Finely chop half the truffle and stir it into the eggs.

In a double boiler or small saucepan with a stainless steel mixing bowl placed on top, bring 1½ inches of water to a simmer. Rub the inside of the top of the double boiler or the bowl with the 2 tablespoons of soft butter. Pour the beaten eggs into the top of the double boiler or the bowl. Over low heat, stir the eggs gently with a wooden spoon or spatula. Cut the 10 tablespoons of cold butter into teaspoon-size pieces and add 2 or 3 at a time while you continue to stir the eggs, adding a little more butter to the eggs every few minutes as the eggs thicken. Slow-cooked eggs can take up to 20 minutes or longer, depending on your patience. This cooking method will not scramble the eggs. Rather, the much-anticipated result is thickened eggs with a sensual and smooth consistency.

Preheat the oven to 300°F.

Place the bread slices on a baking sheet and bake for 15 minutes until crisp. Keep the croutons warm.

Spoon the eggs into warm bowls and finish by shaving the remaining half truffle over them with a peeler. Serve immediately with the warm croutons.

LOUIS DRESSING

ABOUT 2 CUPS

Serve homemade Louis dressing with chilled cracked crab or with crabmeat mounded in a chilled martini glass with wedges of avocado and shredded lettuce.

8 whole good-quality canned roma tomatoes
1 cup Homemade Mayonnaise (page 19)
1 tablespoon fresh lemon juice
1 teaspoon red wine vinegar
1 teaspoon champagne vinegar
1 tablespoon minced shallot
One 9-minute hard-cooked egg (see page 6), finely chopped
1 tablespoon chopped fresh tarragon
1 tablespoon chopped fresh chives
1 tablespoon chopped fennel fronds
2 teaspoons of Worcestershire sauce
Salt to taste
Freshly ground black pepper to taste

Roast the tomatoes on a small sheet pan in a 200°F. oven for 1½ hours, or until the tomatoes have lost their moisture and become "jammy" but not browned. Purée in a food processor or blender until smooth.

To the mayonnaise, add ½ cup of roasted tomato purée with the lemon juice, vinegars, shallot, and hard-cooked egg. Blend well and stir in the chopped herbs. Flavor with the Worcestershire sauce, a pinch of salt, and pepper. Taste and adjust the seasoning, adding more vinegar or salt.

Covered and refrigerated, Louis dressing will keep for 2 days.

BÉARNAISE MAYONNAISE

ABOUT 1 CUP

This is our variation on the classical warm béarnaise sauce.
We made it to accompany a "mile high" rare roast beef sandwich.
Fragrant tarragon complements chicken and vegetables too.

1 cup Homemade Mayonnaise (page 19)
1 tablespoon chopped fresh tarragon
2 tablespoons minced shallot
3 tablespoons champagne vinegar
1 tarragon branch
Salt to taste
⅛ teaspoon freshly ground white pepper

Combine the mayonnaise and tarragon. Set aside. Place the shallot in a small pan with the vinegar, tarragon, and salt. Simmer over low heat until most of the vinegar is evaporated, softening the shallot. Let the shallot cool. Add the shallot mixture to the tarragon mayonnaise. Add the pepper and taste and adjust for salt and vinegar. Covered and refrigerated, the béarnaise mayonnaise will keep for several days.

egg a day

Fresh eggs,
elemental ingredients,
and immediate
cooking techniques
make these five dishes
perfect starts to
bustling weekday —
or even weekend—
mornings.

ALE AND CHEDDAR OMELET

FOR EACH OMELET

The mild hop flavor of light ale combined with eggs is delicate—
the omelet has a lacy texture and an effervescent quality.

¼ cup pale ale or lager
3 eggs
Salt to taste
⅓ cup grated sharp aged Cheddar cheese

Set a 7- to 8-inch nonstick egg pan over high heat and add the pale ale or lager. (Thicker ales and beers will overwhelm the flavor of the eggs.) Let the ale sizzle and reduce by half, about 1 minute.

Beat the eggs and season with salt. Still over high heat, pour in the eggs and let the bottom set slightly, rotating the pan to bring the egg to the edges. Bring the cooked edges of the egg into the center with a wooden spoon or chopstick, letting the raw egg run underneath. Repeat until the bottom layers are set and the top of the omelet is moist and creamy. Add the Cheddar cheese. Begin to roll the cooked side of the egg over the creamy side and the filling. Repeat the rolling motion several times until the cooked side has rolled back onto itself. Flip the omelet to help seal it. Roll the omelet onto a warm plate.

HAM AND DIJON MUSTARD OMELET

FOR EACH OMELET

Browning the butter before pouring in the egg brings out
a nutty flavor that complements the flavors of the ham and Dijon mustard.
For a weekend treat, enjoy this with a glass of fruity Pinot Grigio.

2 eggs
Salt to taste
2 teaspoons Dijon mustard
I tablespoon unsalted butter
I slice country-style ham, cut into strips

Beat the eggs lightly, season with salt, and mix in the mustard. Heat a
7- to 8-inch nonstick or seasoned egg pan until it is very hot and add
the butter. Swirl the butter to coat the bottom and sides of the pan.
After the butter begins to brown slightly, pour in the eggs. Let the
bottom of the egg set slightly and bring the edges of the egg into
the center, letting the raw egg run underneath. Repeat until the bottom
layers are set and the top is moist and creamy. Sprinkle the ham over
the top of the egg. Lift the edge of the omelet with a wooden spoon,
spatula, fork, or chopstick and roll the omelet up over itself. Flip once
to let the omelet seal and set. Roll onto a warm plate.

OEUFS À LA COQUE

FOR TWO

*Sitting in little eggcups, these regal three-minute ready-to-eat
eggs are a cheerful sight in the morning.*

2 slices rustic French bread
Salt to taste
1 tablespoon melted unsalted butter
2 eggs
Freshly ground black pepper to taste

Preheat the oven to 300°F.

Cut the bread into long finger shapes, about $1/2$ inch wide. Place on
a baking sheet, season with a little salt, and drizzle with melted butter.
Bake until the slices are golden brown and crisp, about 12 minutes.

Bring a small saucepan of water to a boil. Gently lower the eggs one
at a time into the water with a spoon to prevent the shells from cracking. Lower the heat and simmer for 3 minutes. Lift the eggs out of the
saucepan and place in eggcups, with the smaller end of the egg up. Let
the eggs rest for a moment. Remove the tips of the eggs with a knife.
Serve the eggs surrounded by warm toast bâtons and pass salt and pepper at the table.

PAN-SCRAMBLED EGGS

FOR TWO

Cracking the eggs directly into the pan and scrambling creates delicately marbled eggs, terrifically tender eggs—and one less bowl to clean.

I tablespoon pure olive oil or unsalted butter
I tablespoon chopped fresh parsley
I tablespoon slivered fresh green onion
3 eggs
Salt to taste
4 slices rustic sourdough bread, toasted
I garlic clove (optional)

In a 7- or 8-inch nonstick or seasoned egg pan, heat the oil or butter. Add the parsley and green onion. Over medium heat, vigorously sauté the parsley-onion mixture until slightly softened and even starting to become a bit caramelized.

Turn down the heat to medium low and crack open the eggs into the pan. Sprinkle with salt. We use a single wooden chopstick to mix the eggs quickly, but a wooden spoon or fork works too. Whirl the eggs and parsley-onion mixture together. Work fast and keep the heat medium low or the eggs will become tough. When the eggs have reached their desired consistency, spread them over the warm toast, lightly rubbed with a garlic clove if desired, and eat like crostini, or open-faced sandwiches.

Steamed Eggs with Vinegar and Herbs

FOR TWO

Plump steamed eggs are lightly mashed onto hot toast and flavored with earthy marjoram and oregano and drops of red wine vinegar.

4 eggs

1 or 2 sprigs fresh marjoram, oregano, or your favorite herb

4 thick slices rustic French bread, toasted

1 teaspoon sherry vinegar

Salt to taste

Freshly ground black pepper to taste

Use nonstick eggcups or rub soft butter to thinly coat the inside of four cups or ramekins. Place 1 egg in each cup or ramekin. Steam covered for 4 minutes, or until the egg whites are cooked and the yolks creamy.

While the eggs steam, pick the leaves of the marjoram or oregano and roughly chop.

Remove the eggs from the cups and place each on a slice of toast. You may need to help ease out the eggs with the tip of a knife. Lightly mash them onto the toast. Sprinkle the eggs with the vinegar, about $1/4$ teaspoon over each egg, and chopped herbs. Pass salt and freshly ground black pepper at the table.

weekend eggs

Late-morning meals
are a weekend luxury,
and here are
half a dozen ways
to indulge yourself
or friends.
All go
well with
the Sunday paper!

ASPARAGUS EGG GRATIN

FOR SIX

You can substitute other vegetables for the asparagus, such as tender stewed
artichokes, sautéed wild mushrooms, or creamed potatoes.
To bake the eggs you need six small ceramic gratin dishes that allow you to
start the eggs on the stove and then finish them in the oven.

¾ pound asparagus
3 tablespoons unsalted butter
I cup heavy cream
Salt to taste
I 2 eggs
⅓ cup freshly grated Parmesan cheese (optional)
6 thin slices prosciutto
Edible flowers (nasturtiums, pansies, borage, or sage—
whatever is in your garden),
roughly chopped, for garnish
2 tablespoons of your favorite chopped herbs, for garnish

Preheat the oven to 350°F.

Trim the ends of the asparagus. Peel the fibrous skin of the spears
with a vegetable peeler. Slice the asparagus on a bias about ¼ inch
thick. Leave some of the smaller tips whole. In a skillet, sauté the
asparagus lightly in 1 tablespoon of the butter. This should be brief,
about 1 minute or less, because the asparagus is sliced thin. Add the

cream to the pan and bring the mixture to a gentle simmer, then quickly remove from the heat. The sweet asparagus will perfume the cream. Season with salt.

Butter six small gratin dishes and crack 2 eggs into each one. Pour ¼ cup or more of the asparagus-cream mixture over each set of eggs. Make sure to get enough of the asparagus into each dish. Gently warm the bottom of each gratin dish over a low burner for about 3 minutes, or until the whites are about half-cooked. Place tiny pieces of the remaining 2 tablespoons of butter on top of the eggs, sprinkle with Parmesan, if using, and finish cooking in the oven for 3 to 5 minutes, depending on how cooked you like the eggs.

Place the gratins on small plates and drape a slice of prosciutto over each gratin. Sprinkle with edible flowers and herbs. Serve with warm toast.

Bagna Cauda Scrambled Eggs

FOR FOUR

*Infuse warm anchovy-garlic sauce into fluffy scrambled eggs
to raise the spirits on sleepy weekends.*

FOR THE BAGNA CAUDA

2 small garlic cloves, peeled

3 anchovy fillets, cleaned

¼ cup heavy cream

¼ cup fruity extra virgin olive oil

2 teaspoons fresh lemon juice

½ teaspoon chopped lemon zest

Freshly ground black pepper to taste

Salt to taste

3 thick slices rustic French bread

I tablespoon pure olive oil

½ teaspoon salt

8 eggs

Make the bagna cauda in a mortar with a pestle. Roughly chop the garlic, then grind, adding an anchovy at a time until the two ingredients are a smooth paste. Slowly pour in the cream and the ¼ cup olive oil, stirring with the pestle to marry the flavors. Transfer the sauce to a small pot and gently warm. Do not boil or reduce. Add the lemon juice, lemon zest, and lots of pepper. Taste for salt and adjust the seasoning, adding more lemon, pepper, garlic, or anchovy. Bagna cauda improves with time and can be made a day or two in advance.

Preheat the oven to 300°F.

Cut the slices of bread into cubes and toss them with the tablespoon of olive oil and the $\frac{1}{2}$ teaspoon of salt. Place on a baking sheet and bake for 15 minutes, or until golden brown. Keep the croutons warm.

Place $\frac{1}{2}$ cup of bagna cauda in a large nonstick pan and heat gently. Beat the eggs lightly and combine with the sauce. Scramble the eggs over low heat, stirring slowly to form large creamy curds. Taste for salt. Spoon the eggs onto warm plates and sprinkle with the warm croutons. Grind black pepper over the eggs and eat at once.

FRENCH TOAST

FOR FOUR

Thick slices of sweet baguette soak thoroughly in the egg mixture for a custardy interior and a golden crisp exterior. Depending on the season, you can garnish the French toast with sautéed apples, fresh berries, peach or nectarine slices, sliced bananas, toasted almonds, powdered sugar, or orange butter.

I day-old baguette

4 eggs

I egg yolk

2 cups milk

I teaspoon vanilla extract

I teaspoon orange flower water (optional)

2 tablespoons sugar

¾ teaspoon salt

2 teaspoons unsalted butter

Slice the baguette on a gentle bias into 20 slices, about ³/₄ inch thick.

Beat the whole eggs, yolk, milk, vanilla, orange flower water, sugar, and salt together, and blend well. Pour the mixture into a shallow dish. Submerge the slices of bread and prick their surfaces with a fork for better absorption. If the bread is fairly dry, turn it over frequently and press the bread into the batter, massaging the batter into the bread. It is important to let the bread sit in the batter for at least 15 minutes before cooking; this ensures a custardlike interior when the bread is cooked.

continued

Melt the butter in a cast-iron skillet or on a seasoned griddle over medium heat. Place the bread slices, in batches, into the foaming butter and turn the heat to low. Cook each piece of bread 3 to 4 minutes on each side, just until the bread is golden brown and the inside is like pudding. If the French toast cooks too long, the surface of the bread becomes tough. Add more butter to the skillet if necessary. Serve on warm plates.

Manny's Lemon "Pancake"

FOR TWO

Spending the night with my best friend, Lucia, at her dad's house always meant one thing: Manny's dramatic egg "pancake" in the morning.

3 eggs
½ cup milk
½ cup all-purpose flour
½ teaspoon salt
3½ tablespoons unsalted butter
Juice of half a lemon
Powdered sugar
Your favorite fruit preserves

Preheat the oven to 375°F.

Whisk the eggs and milk together. Add the flour and salt. Whip until a smooth batter with tiny bubbles is achieved.

Melt the butter in a 10- to 12-inch cast-iron skillet. When the butter is hot and begins to sizzle, pour in the batter. Place the skillet on the middle rack of the oven for 12 to 15 minutes, until the "pancake" is light golden and has risen like a soufflé. The edges will appear to be spilling over the rim of the skillet and be nicely browned.

Remove from the oven, sprinkle with lemon juice, and dust generously with powdered sugar. Cut the pancake into four pieces, serve with your favorite fruit preserves, and eat immediately.

OEUFS SUR LE PLAT

FOR FOUR

Oeufs sur le plat, *the French term for shirred eggs, are whole eggs gently
baked in buttered dishes with cream, cheese, or meat—a handy dish for
doubling when you are expecting a crowd.*

4 tablespoons unsalted butter
4 slices cooked country-style ham
8 eggs
2 tablespoons chopped fresh tarragon or chervil, for garnish
Salt to taste
Freshly ground black pepper to taste
6 to 8 slices French bread, lightly toasted

Preheat the oven to 350°F.

Melt the butter in a large porcelain or enameled cast-iron baking
dish or shallow Spanish *cazuela*. Add the ham slices and brown lightly
on both sides. Cover the bottom of the baking dish with the ham slices.
Crack each egg gently into a small bowl and slide it onto the ham. Cook
over low heat for 3 to 5 minutes, or until the whites are half-cooked.
Finish cooking the eggs in the oven for 3 minutes, or until they are set.
Sprinkle the chopped herbs over the eggs and season with salt and pepper. Serve with the toasted bread slices.

POACHED EGGS IN A POTATO NEST

FOR TWO

Poached eggs are set into pan-crisped potato-onion purée; the potato cakes resemble a bird's nest, crisp and golden.

FOR THE POTATO-ONION PURÉE

5 tablespoons unsalted butter or pure olive oil

¾ cup diced yellow onion

Salt to taste

½ pound peeled Yellow Finnish potatoes, cut into 1-inch pieces

¼ cup water

Milk or cream (optional)

4 eggs

2 tablespoons crème fraîche

Edible flowers (nasturtiums, pansies, or borage), for garnish

In a 2-quart heavy-duty pot, melt 3 tablespoons of the butter or olive oil over high heat and add the onion. Lower the heat to medium low, cover, and cook until tender. Season with a small pinch of salt. Add the potatoes, water, and a large pinch of salt. Turn the heat up to medium. Cover and stir frequently to keep the potatoes from sticking to the bottom of the pot. When the potatoes have completely broken down, stir them until they are creamy. Moisten the potato-onion purée with a little water (or milk or cream) and season to taste. Remove from heat and let the potatoes cool.

continued

After the potatoes are cool, form them into two 4-inch-diameter patties that are 1 inch thick.

Bring 2 to 3 inches of water to a simmer in a heavy sauté pan.

Over medium-high heat, melt the remaining 2 tablespoons of butter or oil in a large nonstick pan or iron skillet. When it is hot, add the potato-onion patties and brown over medium heat until crisp and browned on the bottom, 8 to 10 minutes. Turn the patties over to brown and crisp the other sides, 5 minutes or so; add more butter or oil if necessary.

Meanwhile, poach the eggs in the simmering water for 3 to 5 minutes, depending on desired doneness. Place the potato patties on two warm plates. Lift out the eggs and blot with a towel. With a spoon, separate each patty slightly and make a well in the center. Place 2 eggs in each well.

Drizzle the egg nests with crème fraîche and garnish with edible flowers.

POPOVERS

Crisp outsides and tender middles make popovers irresistible little packages that fill the house with a sweet aroma as they bake. Serve them with several flavors of fruit preserves or spoon warm scrambled eggs into their centers.

2 eggs

1 cup milk

1 scant cup all-purpose flour

1½ teaspoons salt

2 tablespoons melted unsalted butter

1 tablespoon cold unsalted butter

Preheat the oven to 425°F. Place a nonstick muffin tin inside to get hot.

Beat the eggs in a large bowl with the milk. Whisk in the flour, salt, and melted butter. Whisk the batter until blended, but don't overbeat or the eggs will lose their rising power. The batter should have the consistency of heavy whipping cream. For best rising results, bring the batter to room temperature, approximately 70°F. This can be achieved by carefully warming the batter over very low heat for 1 to 2 minutes or by placing the bowl in the sun for 5 minutes.

Remove the hot muffin tin from the oven and grease the cups with a nugget of cold butter attached to a skewer. Pour in the batter so each cup is two-thirds full. (Do not overfill or the popovers will not rise properly.) Bake for 15 minutes. Without peeking, lower the oven temperature to

350°F. and continue to bake for 20 minutes more. The popovers should be golden and at least twice their original volume. For drier popovers, return them to the oven for an additional 5 minutes. Serve the steaming-hot popovers immediately.

TARTAR SAUCE

ABOUT 1½ CUPS

We use hard-cooked egg to enrich the fines herbes, mustard, and shallot flavors. You can also add one anchovy fillet finely chopped or ground until smooth in a mortar. Grilled fish, fried shrimp and squid, homemade onion rings, and french fries are complete in the presence of homemade tartar sauce.

1 heaping teaspoon capers, rinsed

1 cup Homemade Mayonnaise (page 19)

1½ tablespoons cornichons

1 small shallot, finely minced

1 tablespoon red wine vinegar

One 9-minute hard-cooked egg (see page 6)

1 heaping tablespoon fines herbes (combination of fresh chopped tarragon, parsley, chervil, and chives)

1 teaspoon Dijon mustard

Salt to taste

Chop half of the capers, leaving the rest whole, and combine all the capers with the mayonnaise. Chop the cornichons and add to the mayonnaise. Combine the shallot and red wine vinegar and let stand for 10 minutes to lightly pickle and soften the shallot. Finely chop the egg, combine with the fines herbes, and add to the sauce.

Add the macerated shallot and the mustard. Stir the sauce and season with salt.

Tartar sauce will keep up to 2 days tightly covered and refrigerated.

eggs for supper

These recipes inspire impromptu,
nourishing meals when
few ingredients
are on hand. Relax and
savor creamy Eggs with
Gruyère, Mustard,
and Wine (page 96)
in front of the fireplace.
Or, enjoy an intimate dinner
for two with Flash-Fried Eggs (page 97)
nestled into garden lettuces
with croutons.

Braised Chard à la Polonaise

FOR FOUR

The French call the sprinkling of chopped hard-cooked egg and toasted
bread crumbs over cooked vegetables à la polonaise or "like the Polish."
This addictive topping gives favorite vegetables—asparagus, beets, broccoli,
broccoli rabe, cauliflower, spinach, leeks, escarole—rich texture.

½ cup coarse bread crumbs
1 tablespoon melted unsalted butter
Salt to taste
2 to 3 bunches green chard (about 2 pounds)
2 tablespoons extra virgin olive oil
2 tablespoons water
Two 8-minute hard-cooked eggs (see page 6),
peeled and finely chopped

Preheat the oven to 350°F.

Mix the bread crumbs with the butter in a bowl and season with salt. Place on a baking sheet and bake for 10 minutes, or until golden brown. Stir the bread crumbs halfway through the baking process to insure even cooking. Keep warm.

Stem, wash, and drain the chard leaves. Tear or cut the leaves into 1-inch-wide ribbons. Heat the olive oil in a pot large enough to hold all the leaves. Add the chard with the water and season with salt. Cook, covered, over low heat, stirring occasionally to keep the chard cooking evenly. Continue to cook until the chard is very tender, about 20 minutes. Serve on a warm platter, sprinkled with chopped egg and warm toasted bread crumbs.

CHICKEN LIVERS AND RED WINE OMELET

FOR EACH OMELET

Rich chicken livers, robust red wine, and shallots propel this full-flavored omelet to true supper stature. It goes very well with a glass of red wine, warm French bread, and a chicory salad.

3½ teaspoons butter
1 tablespoon slivered shallot
3 tablespoons cleaned and diced chicken livers
Salt to taste
2 tablespoons fruity red wine
3 eggs, lightly beaten

Melt 2 teaspoons of the butter in a 7- or 8-inch nonstick egg pan over low heat. Add the slivered shallot and cook until the shallot is tender. Turn up the heat and add the chicken livers. Sauté for 30 seconds, shaking the pan until the liver bits are seared on all sides. Season with salt. Add the red wine and cook until the wine evaporates. Pour the bits of liver and juice into a bowl with the lightly beaten eggs. Season with salt.

Wipe the pan clean and, over medium-high heat, melt the remaining 1 $\frac{1}{2}$ teaspoons of butter. After the butter foams, add the liver-egg mixture. Pull the sides of the egg into the center as it sets and let the raw egg run underneath and set. Repeat several times, until most of the bottom layers of egg are set, while the top layer remains creamy and moist. Fold the egg over at the edge of the pan and begin to roll up the omelet. Flip the omelet once to secure the roll. Slide the omelet onto a warm plate.

Eggs with Gruyère, Mustard, and Wine

FOR TWO

*A perfect way to use last night's leftover white wine, these
mustard-flavored eggs are a comfort on a dark winter evening.*

½ baguette
I tablespoon melted unsalted butter
I tablespoon cold unsalted butter
¼ cup dry white wine
I ½ teaspoons Dijon mustard
⅓ cup grated Gruyère cheese
4 eggs
Salt to taste
I teaspoon chopped fresh parsley or chives, for garnish

Preheat the oven to 300°F.

Slice the baguette into ⅓-inch slices. Place on a baking sheet and
brush with the melted butter. Bake for 10 minutes, or until golden
brown. Keep the croutons warm.

Combine the cold butter and white wine in a skillet and cook over
medium heat for 2 to 3 minutes, or until the wine is reduced by half.
Remove from the heat. Add the mustard and cheese and stir until the
cheese is melted.

Crack the eggs into a bowl and whip lightly. Season with salt and add
the eggs to the pan. Use a wooden spoon to gently scramble the eggs into

large soft curds. Cook for 1½ minutes, or less if you want softer curds.

Spoon the eggs quickly onto warm plates and serve them with the warm croutons, or insert thin croutons into the eggs for visual flair. Sprinkle with the chopped parsley or chives.

FLASH-FRIED EGGS

FOR TWO

This is a rapid but delicate procedure in which egg whites turn golden while the yolks remain creamy. The kind of oil you choose to fry the eggs in will determine the taste—olive oil for a fruity flavor, lard for a sweeter flavor, and neutral-tasting peanut or corn oil to keep the flavor of the egg unchanged.

4 slices rustic French bread, crusts removed

2 teaspoons melted unsalted butter

1½ cups oil

4 eggs

Salt to taste

Freshly ground black pepper to taste

Few handfuls of garden lettuces

Your favorite vinaigrette

1 teaspoon chopped fresh parsley, chervil, tarragon, or a combination, for garnish

continued

Preheat the oven to 300°F.

Place the bread slices on a baking sheet and brush with the melted butter. Bake for 10 minutes, or until golden. Keep the croutons warm.

In a frying pan or cast-iron pan, heat the oil until it is quite hot, about 325°F. More heat will cause the eggs to be tough and rubbery. Test the oil with a thermometer or by adding a bread cube. The oil should sizzle but not brown the bread. Crack 1 egg into the oil, then tilt the pan quickly to form a well of oil deep enough to immerse the egg. With a spoon, ease the exposed white away from the base of the pan. Gently fold the white over the yolk to enclose it. The layers of white will protect the yolk from the heat. When the egg white appears firm and starts to brown, lift the egg out with a slotted spoon. Let the excess oil drip back into the pan. With a paper towel, blot the egg of excess oil on the top and bottom. Season with salt and pepper. Repeat with the remaining eggs.

Serve the fried eggs on croutons and garden lettuces, sprinkled with your favorite vinaigrette. Garnish with chopped herbs.

PASTA CARBONARA

FOR TWO

Pasta carbonara requires just a few staples: eggs, pasta, bacon, and some Parmesan cheese. Delicately cooked by the heat of the noodles, the egg becomes the binding sauce.

½ pound (or just under) long noodles (linguine, fedelini, or spaghettini)

3 thick slices smoky bacon

I tablespoon pure olive oil

2 eggs

Salt to taste

Chunk of Parmesan cheese, freshly grated

Freshly ground black pepper to taste

Bring slightly salted water to a boil in a large pot. Cook the noodles until tender but firm. While the noodles cook, dice the bacon and cook it in the olive oil until just lightly crisped in a medium sauté pan. Pour off the excess fat, reserving 2 tablespoons in the pan.

In a bowl, beat the eggs and season with a little salt.

Drain the noodles, saving about 1 tablespoon of water for later. If the pan has cooled down, warm it up again right before adding the noodles. Add the noodles to the warm bacon in the pan; thoroughly toss with the oil and bacon, and season with salt. Work fast and pour the beaten egg onto the warm noodles and mix well to coat the noodles.

continued

Add the reserved pasta water if the noodles look dry. The heat of the noodles and the pan will thicken and set the eggs. If there is not enough heat, turn the burner on very low, just to warm the noodles, then turn it off. Too much heat can scramble the eggs.

Once the noodles, egg, and bacon are well mixed, add freshly grated Parmesan cheese and stir. Freshly ground black pepper is an essential addition. Serve in warm pasta bowls.

Roast Chicken Omelet with Fried Croutons

FOR EACH OMELET

Diced roasted chicken and chopped bacon fortify this omelet. The croutons give it texture. Serve with a chilled rosé such as Tavel or Lirac.

2½ tablespoons unsalted butter

⅓ cup hand-cut diced croutons from day-old rustic French bread

Salt to taste

Freshly ground black pepper to taste

¼ cup slivered onion

2 tablespoons diced bacon

3 heaping tablespoons diced roasted chicken

Freshly grated nutmeg

1 teaspoon cooking sherry

2 eggs

Melt 1 tablespoon of the butter in a sauté pan over medium heat. Add the croutons and sauté until golden on all sides. Season with salt and pepper. Set aside and keep warm.

In a small nonstick pan, cook the onion in 1 tablespoon of butter over medium heat until it softens. Add the bacon and cook for 3 minutes, or until just cooked, not crisp. Stir in the chicken. Flavor with nutmeg and the sherry. Remove from the heat.

continued

Beat the eggs in a small bowl; season with salt and add the chicken mixture to the beaten egg. Blend lightly and set aside.

Over high heat, melt the remaining ½ tablespoon of butter in the same pan. When the butter begins to foam, quickly add the egg mixture to sear the bottom layer of egg. Tilt the pan to let the egg run to the edges. Pull the edges to the center to let the raw egg run underneath. As the omelet begins to set, before you begin to roll the omelet, drop in half of the croutons. Then roll the omelet and slide it onto a warm plate. Garnish with the remaining croutons.

SAFFRON EGG AND RICE CAKE

FOR SIX OR MORE

Toasted and ground saffron threads give color to this Persian egg and rice cake. Accompany it with spicy grilled chicken, meat, and vegetables, or lightly fry wedges in olive oil for breakfast.

3 cups basmati rice
2 tablespoons salt plus more to taste
½ teaspoon saffron threads
¼ cup warm water
3 egg yolks
2 cups plain yogurt
Freshly ground black pepper to taste
12 tablespoons unsalted butter

Preheat the oven to 350°F.

Pour the rice into a bowl of warm water. Remove the starch from the rice by rinsing it in five changes of water until the water runs clear.

Bring 10 cups of water to a boil with the 2 tablespoons of salt in a large pot. Boil the cleaned rice in the pot for 5 minutes, stirring frequently so the rice doesn't stick together. Drain in a colander and rinse with warm water. The rice will be tender but not completely cooked.

Toast the saffron threads in a small pan in the oven for 5 to 8 minutes, or until brittle; this will make the saffron easier to grind. Grind the toasted saffron threads into dust in a mortar with a pestle. Dissolve the saffron in the warm water.

continued

Combine the egg yolks, yogurt, saffron, and salt and pepper in a large bowl and mix well. Blend in the rice. Melt 8 tablespoons of the butter in a 9- or 10-inch cast-iron pan. Add the rice mixture to the pan and pack down firmly with a spatula. Melt the remaining 4 tablespoons of butter and pour over the rice. Cover and bake for 1½ hours. Remove the rice cake from the oven and let it rest for 10 minutes with a damp cloth on top. Invert onto a cutting board or platter and slice into wedges.

VIETNAMESE EGG SOUP

FOR TWO OR MORE

Ribbons of egg float in this hot velvety soup studded with pork and shrimp. Simply assemble all the ingredients in a large bowl and steam or microwave.

1 tablespoon chopped fresh green onion

¼ teaspoon sugar

½ teaspoon salt

¼ teaspoon freshly ground black pepper

5 button mushrooms, thinly sliced

3 shiitake mushrooms, stemmed and cut into quarters

3 tablespoons ground pork (optional)

1 fresh medium shrimp, peeled and thinly sliced

2 tablespoons oyster sauce

2 eggs

2 cups water

In a 1-quart ovenproof ceramic bowl or dish, place the green onion, sugar, salt, pepper, mushrooms, pork, if using, shrimp, and oyster sauce. Crack the eggs into the bowl and stir all the ingredients together vigorously with two chopsticks or a fork. Add the water to the egg mixture and cover with foil.

Place the bowl in a steamer on the stove or in a water bath in a 350°F. oven. Steam for 20 to 25 minutes, or until the egg has set. (The bowl can be covered with plastic wrap and placed in a microwave for about 5 minutes.) To determine if the egg is completely cooked, pierce the egg with a knife; the egg should be slightly resistant, and the broth underneath should run clear. Ladle the soup into warm bowls or cups.

Zuppa alla Pavese

A seventeenth-century Italian peasant quickly improvised this rustic soup when an unexpected visit by her battle-ridden Pavian king inspired her to add two newly laid eggs to scalding broth and fried country bread.

5 pounds chicken backs and necks
3½ quarts cold water
2 carrots, peeled
I yellow onion, peeled and quartered
I celery stalk
2 sprigs parsley
I thyme branch
½ bay leaf
4 peppercorns
Salt to taste

8 slices French bread, sourdough bread, or focaccia
Pure olive oil
4 eggs
Freshly grated Parmesan or pecorino cheese, for garnish

Because we are drawn to the poetry of an egg poached in chicken broth, we start with a chicken stock, but vegetable and beef stock work very well too.

In a stainless steel pot, combine the chicken and water. Bring the water to a boil. Reduce the heat to a simmer, skim well, and add the vegetables, herbs, and peppercorns. Simmer for 3 hours uncovered.

Strain the stock through a fine mesh strainer. Moisten an impeccably clean cotton kitchen cloth or linen napkin with water, squeeze it dry, and place it open over the strainer. Strain the broth through the wet cloth filter until the broth runs clear. Repeat the process once or twice as necessary. Season the broth with salt and transfer it to a clean pot.

Fry the bread in olive oil in a skillet over medium heat until golden on both sides.

Bring the broth back up to a full boil, then reduce the heat to a vigorous simmer, but do not let the broth reduce.

Warm four soup bowls in a warm oven. When the bowls are nearly hot, place 2 croutons in each, and crack an egg into each. Slowly ladle the hot broth onto the eggs. Garnish with a generous grating of Parmesan or pecorino cheese.

the after-dinner egg

These dessert recipes show off
the egg in its diverse glory—
baked crisp and light
in Mother's Schaumtortes (page 112),
dramatically risen
in Chocolate Soufflé (page 109),
thickened in sparkling wine
for Sabayon (page 111),
and sweetly puffed
in Soufflé Fritters (page 113).

Chocolate Soufflé

FOR FOUR

*These individual dessert soufflés cook quickly and finish any meal
with rich chocolatey drama.*

6 ounces bittersweet chocolate, cut into small pieces

¼ cup milk

¼ cup plus 1 tablespoon sugar

1 tablespoon Grand Marnier

4 egg yolks

¼ teaspoon cream of tartar

¼ teaspoon salt

5 egg whites

Powdered sugar, for garnish

Preheat the oven to 375°F.

In a double boiler, melt the chocolate pieces with the milk and ¼ cup sugar over low heat. Don't let the mixture get too hot or it may separate. Whisk the melted chocolate until smooth. Whisk in the Grand Marnier. Remove the chocolate from the heat and stir in the egg yolks.

Combine the egg whites, cream of tartar, and salt in a large bowl. Whip the whites, sprinkling in the remaining 1 tablespoon of sugar a little bit at a time. Continue to whip until the sugar is fully incorporated and the whites form stiff, airy peaks.

continued

Lightly fold 2 or 3 tablespoons of whipped egg whites into the chocolate sauce with a spatula. Carefully fold half of the remaining egg whites into the sauce. Then fold in the final half.

Butter four 6- to 8-ounce soufflé ramekins and dust with powdered sugar, removing any residual sugar. Fill each ramekin three-quarters full with the soufflé batter. Place the ramekins on a baking sheet on the middle rack in the oven. Cook for 12 to 15 minutes. The soufflés are cooked when a skewer inserted in the center comes out clean. Place the soufflé ramekins on small plates and sprinkle with powdered sugar.

SABAYON

The sight of this golden frothy dessert whipped up after supper always delights
our guests. The time of year dictates the fresh fruit we serve with it. Berries,
peaches, and nectarines, peeled and sliced thinly, are perfect to float in the
warm sabayon in the summer months. Autumn and winter fruit options are
peeled grapes, poached pears, pomegranate seeds, and quartered figs.

8 egg yolks

6 tablespoons sugar

¾ cup sweet dessert wine or champagne

Combine the egg yolks and sugar in a stainless steel bowl. Whisk in the
wine and place the bowl over a pot with an inch or two of gently simmering water. Turn the heat low to create a light mist that will thicken
the egg. The pot should be deep enough so that the bottom of the bowl
does not touch the water.

Whisk the egg constantly until the mixture thickens, 2 to 3 minutes.
There should be no liquid left at the bottom of the bowl. Remove from
the heat.

Serve in martini, aperitif, or old-fashioned champagne glasses.

MOTHER'S SCHAUMTORTES

ABOUT TEN LARGE COOKIES

Mother baked pretty meringues for me as a child, just as her German grandmother and mother had. These billowy rounds are made with granulated, not powdered, sugar, which creates crisp, melt-in-your-mouth exteriors with soft, chewy centers. Schaumtortes can also be the base of the lovely Pavlova dessert, which is topped with whipped cream and fresh fruit.

6 egg whites
I teaspoon vanilla extract
⅛ teaspoon cream of tartar
1½ cups sugar

Preheat the oven to 250°F. Line two baking sheets with parchment paper or clean brown paper bags.

Combine the egg whites, vanilla, and cream of tartar in a mixing bowl. Using an electric mixer, beat on high until the whites are frothy. Continue to beat the whites on high, adding the sugar 1 tablespoon at a time, until stiff peaks form. The egg whites will look glossy and the sugar will still be crunchy. Use two spoons to form 4-inch rounds with small peaks and place on the baking sheets.

Bake the schaumtortes for 1 hour and 15 minutes. Turn off the oven and allow them to cool for 5 minutes with the oven door propped open.

SOUFFLÉ FRITTERS

FOR FOUR TO SIX

*Making dessert fritters for friends is worth the effort. The action becomes
the party—dropping the dough in the oil, watching the shapes double in
size, then eating the hot, crisp fritters!*

1 cup milk
⅛ teaspoon salt
¼ teaspoon sugar
8 tablespoons unsalted butter
1 tablespoon brandy
1 teaspoon vanilla extract
1 cup all-purpose flour
4 eggs
2 cups peanut or vegetable oil
¼ cup powdered sugar, for garnish

Heat the milk, salt, sugar, butter, brandy, and vanilla in a saucepan. As
soon as the liquid boils, add the flour. Put the pan on the side of the
burner and quickly beat the mixture well with a wooden spoon until it
is smooth and starts to leave the sides of the pan, without sticking to the
spoon. Remove the pan from the heat and break the eggs into it, one at
a time, beating the batter until smooth after adding each egg. The dough
should be soft but not runny. Let the dough rest, covered, for 1 hour or
refrigerate overnight.

continued

Heat the oil in a deep skillet or heavy-duty pot to 325°F. Line a baking sheet with paper towels. Use two spoons to shape the dough into small irregular-shaped balls about the size of a shelled walnut. If they are larger, the fritters will not cook well in the center. Drop them into the oil a few at a time. Use tongs to turn the fritters over as they brown. Each fritter will take about 2½ minutes to cook in the hot oil. Drain them on the paper towels. Serve them at once, sprinkled with powdered sugar.

Index

E

eggs, fresh, 2

F

fennel and steamed mussels frittata, 51–52
flash-fried eggs, 97–98
French toast, 83–84
fresh eggs, 2
fried eggs:
    balsamic, 57
    bread crumb, 58–59
    croque-madame, 62–63
    in duck fat, 16–17
    flash-, 97–98
    green pepper sandwich, 48
    wild mushrooms "sunny-side up," 26–27
frittatas:
    squash blossom and zucchini, 42–43
    steamed mussels and fennel, 51–52
fritters, soufflé, 113–14

G

garden herbs, mascarpone omelet with, 20
gougères, 45–46
gratin, asparagus egg, 79–80
gratinéed deviled eggs, 46–47
green pepper "fried" egg sandwich, 48
Gruyère, eggs with mustard, wine and, 96–97

H

ham:
    and Dijon mustard omelet, 74
    and egg croquettes, 17–18
hard-cooked eggs:
    and beet salad, 64–65
    braised chard à la polonaise, 93–94

cooking tips for, 6
gratinéed deviled eggs, 46–47
ham and egg croquettes, 17–18
macaroni and egg salad, 36–37
Nanny's sweet pickled egg salad, 49
pickled herring and, 24–25
tartar sauce, 90–91
watercress salsa, 25–26
herbs:
    garden, mascarpone omelet with, 20
    steamed eggs with vinegar and, 77
herring, pickled, and hard-cooked
    egg, 24–25
homemade mayonnaise, 19
huevos à la flamenco, 34–35

J

jam omelet, apricot, 11
Japanese savory custard, 65–66

L

lemon "pancake," Manny's, 85–86
livers, chicken, and red wine
    omelet, 94–95
Louis dressing, 70–71

M

macaroni and egg salad, 36–37
Manny's lemon "pancake," 85–86
mascarpone omelet with garden herbs, 20
mashed potato–baked eggs, 21–22
mayonnaise:
    béarnaise, 71
    homemade, 19
Mother's schaumtortes, 112

mushrooms, wild, "sunny-side up," 26–27
mussels, steamed, and fennel
    frittata, 51–52
mustard:
    Dijon, and ham omelet, 74
    eggs with Gruyère, wine and, 96–97

N

Nanny's sweet pickled egg salad, 49

O

oeufs à la coque, 75
oeufs sur le plat, 86
omelets:
    ale and cheddar, 73
    apricot jam, 11
    caramelized apple, 12–13
    chicken livers and red wine, 94–95
    cooking tips for, 3
    ham and Dijon mustard, 74
    mascarpone, with garden herbs, 20
    onion and cider, 22–23
    potato egg torta, 50–51
    roast chicken, with fried croutons, 101–2
    sorrel, 40–41
onion:
    and cider omelet, 22–23
    -potato purée, 87–88

P

"pancake," Manny's lemon, 85–86
pan-scrambled eggs, 76
pasta:
    carbonara, 99–100
    macaroni and egg salad, 36–37

pepper, green, "fried" egg sandwich, 48
pesto scrambled eggs, 37–38
pickled egg salad, Nanny's sweet, 49
pickled herring and hard-cooked egg, 24–25
pipérade, 39–40
poached and steamed eggs:
    bread crumb fried eggs, 58–59
    cooking tips for, 4
    dandelion salad with a poached
        egg, 14–15
    poached eggs in a potato nest, 87–88
    steamed eggs with vinegar and herbs, 77
    zuppa alla pavese, 106–7
popovers, 89–90
potato:
    egg torta, 50–51
    mashed, -baked eggs, 21–22
    nest, poached eggs in, 87–88
    -onion purée, 87–88

R

rice and egg saffron cake, 103–4
roast chicken omelet with fried
    croutons, 101–2

S

sabayon, 111
saffron egg and rice cake, 103–4
salads:
    dandelion, with a poached egg, 14–15
    egg and beet, 64–65
    macaroni and egg, 36–37
    Nanny's sweet pickled egg, 49
    salmon, smoked, egg, and asparagus
        sandwich, 67–68
salsa, watercress egg, 25–26